KNOW YOUR
DOG

DR DAVID SANDS

KNOW YOUR
DOG

Understand how your dog thinks and behaves

Bounty
BOOKS

First published in Great Britain in 2008 by
Hamlyn, a division of Octopus Publishing Group Ltd

This edition published in 2010 by Bounty Books,
a division of Octopus Publishing Group Ltd
Endeavour House
189 Shaftesbury Avenue
London WC2H 8JY

www.octopusbooks.co.uk

An Hachette UK Company
www.hachette.co.uk

ISBN: 978-0-753721-10-0

A CIP catalogue record for this book is available
from the British Library

Printed and bound in China

The advice given in this book should not be used as a substitute
for that of a veterinary surgeon.

In this book, unless the information is given specifically for female dogs,
dogs are referred to as 'he'. The information is equally applicable to both
male and female dogs, unless otherwise specified.

Contents

Introduction

Man and the dog, a wolf subspecies, have made a very long journey together over a period of thousands of years, which has resulted in a special symbiosis between them. We offer each other such mutual benefits as sociability, protection and food, but perhaps most importantly, dogs of all shapes and sizes offer us a therapeutic relationship. Dogs can help us through times of real struggle and yet they are usually content enough to share in our enjoyment in times of pleasure.

Observing dogs demonstrating their various instinctive skills has been a continual source of fascination for me, in the knowledge that these behaviours have been fine-tuned over millions of years, and I can understand why some anthropologists believe that man evolved faster by hunting alongside the earliest tamed wolves. This fascination coupled with my daily work dealing with problems in dogs and other companion animals has spurred me on to achieve a fuller understanding of dog behaviour. Both the 'disturbed' and 'secure' canine personalities that I have encountered have left an equally lasting impression on my mind.

I am frequently asked which breed out of the amazing range in existence is the ideal one to keep. Years ago, I would have cheerfully declared the Boxer without hesitation, because my family kept some great characters that proved to be entirely dependable with young children. However, I tried to compensate the dreadful loss of a yearling Boxer to a genetic heart defect by replacing him with a mature, powerfully built specimen. This dog displayed what seemed to me at the time to be alien canine behaviour, which I now realize was triggered by the break in his attachment to his previous owner. Nowadays, I see a charm in every breed. Dogs are just like people in that there is the potential for good and bad in every individual.

It has genuinely been both a joy and a challenge to write about the dog purely based around the mechanisms of its behaviour. I cannot shy away from the fact that I am the first to diagnose inappropriate 'humanization' when coming into contact with owners who treat their dogs as though they are children. Yet ironically, I can also see a great many parallels between humans and dogs. We both react to stress in similar ways, and dogs and people always respond best to kindness and understanding.

I invite all dog owners, from those who own active working breeds to others who keep their dogs as close household companions, to view this book with an open mind, on the understanding that they remain the true experts when it comes to knowing their own particular dogs. Here I have examined both the dog's fundamental innate behaviour as well as learned behaviours in an informed light, in my quest to explain how and why they occur and to reveal why our relationship is unique in the animal kingdom. If our knowledge of man's best friend can be enhanced in any way through this exploration, then my aims will have been met.

Right: Dogs reflect fundamental breed traits both in their personalities and displayed skills, and many gundog breeds enjoy the instinct to retrieve, whether it be a game bird or a ball.

Understanding your dog

Behavioural ancestry

In order to appreciate fully your pet dog's behaviour, it is important to know that the canine family includes all species of foxes, wolves, coyotes, dholes, raccoon dogs, jackals and the dingo as well as domesticated dogs. Furthermore, following DNA research, all dogs, from the bear-sized Newfoundland to the tiny Chihuahua, can now be regarded as a subspecies of the wolf.

Above: The retrieval of game birds is a trait that has been selected for and line bred in gundog breeds, such as spaniels.

Wolf ancestry

The Japanese, Chinese, Eastern Timber and Indian wolf have each in their own evolutionary history provided the gene pool that has resulted in all modern dog types and their respective behaviours. Because of their close genetic relationship, domesticated dogs can interbreed with wolves, coyotes and jackals and produce fertile offspring. This interrelationship and gene pool means that dogs have a unique genetic make-up that allows them to be physically modified through breeding. All breeds can be selectively bred over a few generations for small or large body size. This adaptability is clearly illustrated in Poodles, which vary in size from the Standard to the compact Miniature and the even smaller Toy Poodle.

The oldest-known breeds

One of the first breeds to be domesticated is the Dingo in Australia, which has been in existence for at least 8,000 years. The Alaskan Malamute dates back to 3000 BC, and shares much of the same gene profile as the oldest of European breeds, such as those magnificent giants, the Great Dane and European Mastiff, bred to hunt or guard. The all-conquering Roman army were known to use these latter breeds, which have been dated from 2000–1000 BC. The Japanese hunting dogs Shiba Inu and Ainu date back to a similar period, but the Canaan Dog from Israel, dated 2000 BC, and the Cardigan Welsh Corgi, 1200 BC, are thought to be among the oldest herding dogs. The diminutive Maltese, dated 500 BC, is regarded as the oldest of all the toy breeds.

The oldest breeds still carry the most distinctive behavioural traits that help form the backbone of the ten main dog types we know today (see below). It is these remarkable dogs, travelling alongside armies, explorers and immigrants to other countries, and several thousand years of selective breeding that have resulted in the incredible variety of modern dog breeds.

Breed groups

Current DNA research points to ten natural dog groups and each appear to possess a fundamental instinctive behaviour. These are:

Livestock-herding and guardian dogs Breeds that are excellent at displaying circling, stalking and controlling behaviours, parallel to wolves when they are hunting. Training prevents natural predatory behaviour.

Gundogs Breeds that are outstanding in their secondary behavioural role of locating, recovering or pointing out game for humans to complete the primary task.

Scent hounds Breeds that are adept at tracking down game and then use vocalizing behaviour to announce their find.

Sight hounds Breeds that pursue prey and then display predatory behaviour.

Mastiff and Great Dane protective dogs Breeds that are naturally strong and powerful, and display behaviour that is ideal for guarding and fighting.

Bulldogs Breeds that are muscular and strong-boned, and can demonstrate a strength and tenacity that belies their size.

Husky or pulling dogs Breeds that show great strength particularly from the front or girth, and display instinctive pack behaviour.

Terriers going to ground or vermin-control dogs Small to medium breeds that are quick and tenacious, especially in pest-control tasks.

Companion or lap dog breeds All representatives of these breed groups have produced smaller versions that have become popular the world over as close companions and even fashion 'accessories'. They show signs of dependency that make them especially attractive to their owners.

Independent hunting dogs Breeds including the African Basenji and Australian Dingo that do not require nurturing, interaction with or instruction from humans but will hunt alongside them.

CONTINENTAL INFLUENCE

Both existing knowledge and ongoing research regarding the origins of our modern-day dog breeds suggest that the older or primitive types from the colder Northern regions are more likely to have a Husky, thick-coated appearance, and will usually be more socially aware and possess powerful physical attributes to equip them for pulling sledges. In contrast, those breeds from Southern climes tend to be smaller, fine-haired, bush-dog types.

Below: Beagle packs represent one of the best known of the scent hound breeds, used for hunting for many centuries. Their loud, deep baying announces their find.

Above: Huge-boned breeds, such as this St Bernard, reflect one of the largest scales of physical development seen in dogs.

THE SMALL AND THE TALL

A recent major study has revealed that there is a variation to a particular regulatory sequence in a growth gene (part of the canine genome). All small breeds are said to have this variant. In contrast, tall, ancient hunting breeds, including the iconic Great Dane and the lion-hunting Rhodesian Ridgeback, are big boned and long limbed with muscles that are large and strong enough to carry their huge frames.

Anatomy

The dog is naturally designed to chase in short bursts, with the muscular strength to drag down, bite and chew prey. While the internal anatomy of all breeds is similar, there is great variation in the thickness and length of bone and muscle, since dogs have been line bred for different tasks – the very small for vermin control; the large for hunting and working. So size can indicate key behavioural traits.

Skull, jaws and teeth
The skull of the dog shows three basic variations:

1 Long-nosed or dolichocephalic breeds, including scent- and sight-orientated hounds and collies.

2 Short-nosed or brachycephalic breeds, such as livestock-controlling Boxers and Bulldogs.

3 The mesicephalic skull outline, which includes breeds that fall somewhere in between.

All dogs possess elongated jaws, carrying rows of teeth that erupt at different times in their physical development. These have evolved to both rip and chew. The two lines of molar and premolar teeth at the back of the mouth enable the chewing of tough prey flesh and bone. Two front sets of canine and incisors – permanent in the adult dog – are flesh-ripping teeth.

Saliva and sweat
Saliva has a number of important roles to play. A wide mouth offers a dog improved breathing when he is overheated, and the abundance of saliva not only helps to clean his tongue, but its lubricating quality facilitates the swallowing of food. Saliva also carries enzymes necessary for breaking down food as it makes its journey down into the stomach. When a dog's body temperature increases and he holds out his large tongue and repeatedly pants, this allows him to expose his respiratory area to the surrounding cooler air, thus aiding the evaporation of saliva to discharge heat.

Dogs have that distinctive 'doggy' smell because they possess sweat glands distributed across the body to allow the skin to breathe in much the same way as human armpits. These are known as apocrine glands and are not so much for heat regulation as to aid the release of body moisture, and include special bacteria that help to break down sweat. They are also located between the toes to prevent the pads from drying out. These are especially important in extreme heat, where dry pads would leave feet sore and vulnerable to increased cracking and infection.

Fur and skin

The nature of a dog's coat can vary significantly: coarse and wiry, as in the Airedale Terrier; dense and deep, as in the Husky; smooth and fine, as in the Dobermann Pinscher; feathered and waterproof, as in the Golden Retriever; and even hairless, as in the dogs of Mexico and Peru. Fine-coated dogs shed hairs in the warmer months, then increasingly grow them on the onset of cold weather. Wiry-coated dogs lose few hairs and as a result need occasional coat trimming.

A dog's skin has the same inner or dermis layer as humans, but the epidermis or outer layer is much thinner because his 'fur coat' offers him the necessary additional protection. The outer skin includes numerous sebaceous glands that secrete natural oil that acts both as waterproofing and to prevent the coat from drying out. The sebum or oil in the skin helps to insulate the dog against extreme temperature changes.

Deep in a dog's coat are hair follicles producing keratin, required not only for the production of hair but also hard nails, nose skin and footpads. Hair follicles grow and develop to fulfil different roles, including forming a soft undercoat throughout the body. Others form individual guard hairs that make up the coarse outer coat. When a dog displays aggression, the fur around his neck and back thickens as follicle muscles raise the hackles or hairs.

Below: *Most terrier breeds have tough, short coats that require occasional trimming and shed fewer hairs.*

The senses

Your dog will use all his senses in his daily life, but some are sharper and more finely tuned than others. While he can instantly smell and hear a wider range of scents and sounds in the world around him better than you can, he can see and understand much less.

Eyes

Your dog's hearing and scenting take precedence over what he can see, and enable him to detect the movement of prey. This evolved from when his ancestors hunted in minimal light from dusk to dawn. Dogs have three eyelids: upper and lower, as we have, but with an additional third eyelid or membrane. This keeps the eyes moist and also cleans the surface. Under the surface there are hidden cell structures that have evolved to detect the slightest prey movement. Dogs may have had only a split second to find their life-saving evening meal, so the ability to detect something moving is more valuable than having a detailed picture of the world around them. They see mainly in monochrome and perhaps secondary, watered-down colours.

Dog's eyes have a secondary use in body language. When a dog stares at another dog or even at a person and attempts to force eye contact, this is usually a sign of confrontation. In nature, a dog lower in the hierarchy would always try to avoid making direct eye contact with those higher up in the pack. He would often show a displaced behaviour first, such as self-grooming, and look away to show his disinterest in the potential for confrontation. This prevents unnecessary aggression that would leave the pack vulnerable if members were injured in hierarchal conflicts.

Nose

A dog's nose, especially within its large sensory region, has a primary use to enable him to track and detect prey through scent. He can also detect when a female is ready for mating, not only from her body but also from any urine trails. He can smell where other males have been in a territorial sense and can then over-mark where they have left behind urine and faeces trails. Your dog can almost 'taste' food with his nose before he takes a bite.

Above: *With ears held erect this German Shepherd is alert to any new and unusual sounds he may encounter.*

Left: *An alert look and healthy nose show that all this dog's senses are working together to interpret scents, sounds and movement in an instant.*

Ears

While there is a great deal of variation in ear shape, all dogs share an ability to detect a wide range of sounds, and higher frequencies than humans. If there is someone at your door, your dog's head may be cocked to one side and his ears pricked forward and held alert. He is able to direct his ears towards a sound of interest to check out what is going on. At other times when he is at rest, his ears might be still and folded down. When frightened or wary, his ears are quickly pulled right back or up for alertness, to help him avoid conflict and injury. By changing the position of his ears, your dog can also communicate his intended behaviour towards other dogs.

Taste

Dogs don't possess the same number of taste buds as we do; it is estimated that we have 16 times the sensitivity. This difference is most likely because a dog's tongue has other more vital uses, foremost the discharging of heat through excess saliva (see page 12).

Taste buds help us detect differences in sweetness and sourness or bitter and salty food, but this is far less important for a carnivore. Look at the size of your dog's tongue – it is like a tool for pulling food straight into his mouth and on to his powerful jaws lined with strong teeth. When he is hungry, there is little time to taste what is going down!

SNIFFER DOGS

Dogs possess a larger number of sensory cells in the brain, which facilitate a far higher level of scent recognition than we have. When moist and healthy, your dog's nose quickly absorbs scents around him that help stimulate these sensory cells. So highly tuned is this sensory area that 'sniffer dogs' have been trained to locate an amazing range of smells: explosives, drugs, lost or trapped people and even honey in hidden bumble bee nests – making them an invaluable aid to interviews.

Below: Out in the open a dog will detect and identify a wide range of smells, enabling him to track his prey over great distances if necessary.

The thinking dog

Your dog may appear to be intelligent and he probably is when it comes to getting his own way, but his small brain size means that he is not capable of making complex decisions or forming a full understanding of how our social world operates. However, his excellent memory and canine social skills help him relate to all other animals.

Memory ability

Your dog's brain is mainly 'wired' for flight or fight like ours, to help in times of difficulties (see pages 24–25), but it is basic memory or cognitive ability that takes up most of the available space for activity. This means that his behaviour is mostly related to identifying and living with members of his own social group. In your home, this memory ability is reflected in how each human family member has differing needs of him and he of them. His memory banks are also necessary for identifying scents, trails or landmarks, and all other important learning experiences in his daily life. On walks, when he sees another dog, a person or another animal, his thought processes may be fully committed to checking them out and identifying them either by sight or by scent. The most fundamental questions in his mind are likely to be: 'Are they part of my social group or outsiders?', 'Are they a threat or a non-threat?', 'Are they predator or prey?'.

Checking out other dogs

These questions may appear very basic and obvious, but when answered they allow further investigation without taking high risks. When another dog has been sighted, your dog may want to gain basic information that comes from around its genital and anal regions. This is where his powerful sense of smell offers him a fast way to gather extremely important answers such as sex, oestrus cycle and possibly social ranking.

But first, before sniffing to check out such intimate details, he will need to check out the other dog's vocal and body language. If a growl is sounded, this is a clear distance warning telling him to be careful. In physical terms, at both ends of the body there is immediate information pertaining to your dog's personal safety to gather. If the other dog's ears are relaxed and a wagging tail goes from side to side (this is a two-way signal on the part of both dogs), a closer, or investigating, approach can be safely made for a little mutual or social sniffing. Dogs, as we know, will happily check out each other's rear end in this manner. However, if the other dog is rigid, with his ears standing erect and the tail extended, there is a real chance of confrontation.

Two-legged encounters

If it is an approaching person that needs to be checked out, your dog may wait for a visual or vocal invitation. Dog-friendly people usually welcome other people's dogs in a bright tone of voice and may even offer a welcoming knee pat or a friendly hand. If the person begins to chat to you, your dog will take your pause as a signal to sniff them out. More tail wagging from your dog will usually provide some social patting and stroking on the person's part. You may prefer to think of your dog as a genius, but it is more likely that instinct and social behaviour give him a head start.

Above: Our companion animals have an instinctive ability to relate to one another through similar body language.

Right: When greeting each other, dogs quickly scent important details through mutual sniffing.

WHAT IS MY DOG THINKING WHEN HE ENCOUNTERS THE WORLD AROUND HIM?

When a dog is exploring a new environment on a walk and encountering other animals or people in a park or rural area, his brain utilizes all his senses to record landmarks, scents and wildlife, all to be recalled if he should return to the same place.

Sociability

Have you ever wondered why your dog blends in so easily with your family? The simple answer is that he has the ideal instinct to want to be part of a social group. In nature, when dogs or wolves group together in packs, they cooperate, and this aspect of behaviour is extremely important when it comes to hunting for prey food.

Evolutionary background

Almost all the canines have evolved to hunt and live together in groups. This means that, unlike cats, which are solitary predators feeding mainly on small mammals, dogs and wolves are able to hunt not only for small prey but also much larger animals. By working together in a social group, there is more food to be shared and they can also select a suitable mate more easily.

Pack structure

Most wild groups of dogs or wolves have a clearly defined pack structure. The leaders, known as *alpha* males or females, are usually the strongest members, and potential leaders will often have established their position in the social hierarchal system early on in their lives. There will have been instances of point scoring with the onset of sexual maturity. The first physical challenge may have been over remnants from a kill, and in a vigorous tug of war, the strongest will have won the prize. He or she may then bury or eat the 'winnings', but the minor skirmish will have helped to establish who was to be a *beta* male or female or even bottom of the pack, known as *omega*. In the absence of a male leader, the *alpha* female assumes the role of pack leader.

Leadership language

In the wild, *alpha* leadership is clearly demonstrated through subtle and not so subtle etiquette behaviour: which dog eats first, which takes up a higher physical terrain position or which dog leads hunting and foraging episodes. Other leadership clues include which dog has the best resting position near to the den entrance and which high-ranking male the *alpha* female selects as her mate.

High or low status is illustrated through interaction. Lower-pack members might show submissive behaviour to a pack leader by rolling over and exposing a belly, and, on occasions, urinating in a form of fear submission. Younger members might play bow before a high-ranking individual and will often lick a successful hunter leader around the mouth or the neck. Most of the lower-pack members will self-groom or look away rather than have direct eye contact with an *alpha*. They will certainly move away quickly from a kill after one growl or deadly stare from the leader. These pack members never want confrontation and to risk injury unless they have little option but to do so, such as when driving off or killing a pack outsider.

The family – canine pack

Your dog probably knows his place in your family – the equivalent of his canine pack. To most dogs, you will be the pack leader and he will assume a subdominant role. You will eat and then decide to feed him too. You will lead the hunting and foraging episodes because it is you who will decide where and when a walk will take place. You will normally have the most comfortable bed in the house, unless he is allowed to share it. Thankfully, your dog will be able to read these signs of your natural leadership. Most dogs are happy to accept a subdominant role to their owner. They rarely want responsibility and mostly accept the benefits of being subservient and welcome the stability and reassurance that comes with knowing their place in the family hierarchy.

Above left: By living in defined packs with strong leaders, wolves can hunt and forage more efficiently than individuals.

Right: Dogs that are obedient to instructions naturally accept that their owners are pack leaders.

ARE YOU PACK LEADER?

Take a candid look at your dog's behaviour towards you and ask whether he considers you or him to be pack leader. Is he always willing to respond to your instructions? Does he show obedience when you call him? With the observations from nature detailed above in mind, does your dog submit to or challenge you?

A testing dog may want to sit in your chair, or he may growl at you when he has food or sneak off to sleep on your bed. He may also drag you along on his walks. This dog is failing to recognize his owner as pack leader. Consequently, just like a naughty child or moody youngster, he needs to learn what his lower position is by being offered structure and boundaries in his daily family life.

Personality

You no doubt recognize that your dog has a unique personality, but have you ever wondered what particular factors shape your dog's character? To understand his own particular behaviour in daily life, it is important to consider how his breed and age influence him, and the potential effect of nature over nurture.

Personality type

How would you describe your dog's overall personality? Is he:

- slightly introverted; rather reserved, quiet and sensitive?
- gentle and affectionate?
- proud and on the dignified side?
- confident, alert, independent and aloof or haughty?
- extrovert and very enthusiastic; maybe energetic?
- feisty, tenacious, strong-willed and a little bold?

If he is not faithful, obedient and very biddable, perhaps he doesn't fall into any of these types? How is a dog's personality formed? What makes him the dog you have come to know and love so well? The fundamental factors involved are explored below and on pages 22–23.

Life stages

Your dog's personality, much the same as your own, will change with age. In dogs and in humans, personalities are formed at birth, but are shaped through experience. In his youth, your dog will be fresh and brimming with enthusiasm and vitality. Then will come adulthood, which is when he will show his full strength of temperament and staying power. By the time he reaches middle and old age, your dog's personality will to a degree reflect the kind of life he has experienced. He will, hopefully, be wiser, and taking life much more slowly.

Positive early influences

Research involving Labrador litters has helped to illustrate that the early litter period, between one and eight weeks of age, can be extremely influential in forming the way a puppy develops in terms of his personality and behaviour. Puppies with calm and healthy litter-mothers, especially those that are allowed to remain with her for the first eight weeks after birth, are more likely to develop a healthy personality and are less likely to become over-dependent on their owners (see pages 114–115).

Above: Many working breeds form a powerful bond with their owners in the post-litter period, developing a faithful and affectionate personality.

A relaxed mother that has strong maternal instincts will care for and feed her puppies. She will teach them to urinate and defecate outside the nesting box after the first week or reflex period when the puppies are blind and deaf. This behaviour has an important influence later on when it comes to house-training a young puppy. The mother will also deflect any excessive or continual demands for her attention. She will deliberately keep in check any continual mouthing demands for her milk, a behaviour that is not healthy when allowed to get out of control, especially in a large litter.

Above: A calm litter-mother will produce happy and healthy puppies with good behavioural characteristics that will set them up for adulthood.

Negative effects on puppies

Removal of the puppies prior to eight weeks of age and particularly before six weeks of age is known to create behavioural problems in later life for the fast-developing puppies. They need this important early phase to learn social interaction with siblings and accept control from the mother. There can be an adverse affect on puppy behaviour if the mother is ill or distressed during this social period. This is especially the case if people find themselves having to take over the mother's social role in terms of bottle feeding and keeping the puppies warm and secure.

It is known that puppies that remain with their mother for an extended period, particularly beyond the first eight weeks, will begin to form increased attachments both to the mother and the breeder. This can lead to challenges for the new owner, who may find such a puppy displaying over-dependent behaviour from an early stage (see pages 114–115). It is accepted that the correct age to remove a puppy from its litter-mother and siblings is eight weeks. At this stage its early socialiazation is complete, the mother will have checked any over-demanding for food and attention and excessive mouthing. The puppy is then ready to take on his new role as a companion for an owner. Thankfully, puppies are extremely adaptable and most make the transition from the litter period to a new home without any major problems.

Above: Following a natural instinct, sight hounds, such as Greyhounds, are triggered into chase behaviour when they detect the movements of hares and rabbits.

Breed and personality

All dogs possess a breed-influenced personality, even mongrels where there can be a shared personality but one is usually dominant over the others. Breed-specific behaviour can be seen in the representatives of the ten breed groups (see pages 10–11), and if you own a working breed, some knowledge of these can be useful in understanding your dog's type.

Controlling

When not being employed to round up sheep, Border Collies together with Belgian and German Shepherd Dogs, as with all livestock-controlling or guarding breeds, have a particularly strong behavioural instinct that includes circling, which is frequently shown towards family members when out on walks. They respond to a thrown ball by returning, dropping the ball, taking the down (or pause) position and then eyeing the ball in readiness for the next throw. For these dogs, gaining eye contact with an owner and demonstrating their 'work' ethic is a big part of their personality. Many will behave in a near-hyperactive way, running across fields and zigzagging along walks. They are ready for walks as often as their owners are willing to take them.

Tenacity

Which terrier owner hasn't seen his dog take a very firm hold of a rag or a toy and then proceed to shake it vigorously with much growling and snarling? Such talent is a necessity when the working terrier is being instructed to seek out and kill an unwanted mouse or rat. These breeds are always nosing down into any hole or burrow, so are often seen in similar mode in the home, head first under the sofa, as they keenly search for that lost squeaky toy.

Mouthing

Gundog breeds, including Labradors and other retrievers, spaniels, setters and pointers, show a tendency to approach and greet an owner by mouthing a favourite toy, in effect

KILLER INSTINCT?

One of the behavioural reasons why terriers enjoy attacking dog toys that make a noise is that they are 'killing the mouse' if they silence the squeak. Terriers such as the Staffordshire and English Bull have a distant history of fighting and badger- and bull-baiting, which may encourage them to behave aggressively. Nonetheless, individuals of these breeds can also display a loyalty and protectiveness that endear them to their owners.

saying 'Look what I have found and brought for you', while furiously wagging their tails. They are usually biddable and faithfully willing to take handling instructions. Gentler members of these breeds have a naturally soft mouth that can carry any item (even if it isn't a game bird) with the utmost care. Some extroverted individuals are prone to mouth the hands of owners. These breeds possess a reservoir of energy.

Seeing or smelling

Single-minded scent hounds, such as the Bloodhound, Dachshund, Beagle and Basset, can offer an owner a rather disinterested glance when instructed to do the simplest task, yet when out on walks, as soon as they are stimulated by an interesting animal scent, they will put their determination to use as they set out to track it down. This scenario is very often performed to the sound of despairing calls from an owner, as they helplessly watch their dog speeding across a field and disappearing into a dense thicket. Sight hounds are similarly stimulated by something that catches their eye. Breeds such as Greyhounds and Whippets or the Saluki and Borzoi need only to see potential prey for them to set chase until it is lost or caught.

Stubbornness

Dominance and stubbornness come naturally to the large and powerful, strong-willed breeds such as the Mastiff types. The Bulldog and Boxer types are the same in behavioural terms but without the vertical stature. If a companion Bulldog regards the weather outside as too wet, he will simply sit down on his strong rump and haunches, using all his considerable upper strength, dig his paws into the ground and refuse to go anywhere. That same stubbornness was very useful a century ago when the task of the working Bulldog or Boxer would have been to bite at the heels of unruly heavier livestock until they went in the required direction. That said, the Bulldog, Boxer and Mastiff can also show a loyalty that owners wouldn't swap for any other breed.

Below: A Collie's instinct to circle and wait in the pause, or down, position originates in their natural ability to control and herd livestock.

Fight, freeze or flight

One of the most fascinating aspects of your dog's behaviour can be observed when he instinctively reacts towards unusual circumstances and when he is exposed to new events that test his survival skills. One of the most primary instincts in all vertebrate animals is known as the 'fight or flight response'.

PRIMITIVE POWER

The fight or flight response involves the hormone noradrenaline, which immediately signals to the brain to bring adrenaline into action. These particular hormones are known to affect how animals, including humans, react when placed in situations where there is a sense of danger, pain or fear, making muscles work even harder than they normally would in order to aid escape or to fuel strength and aggression for defence. Secondary effects of the fight or flight response include the stimulation of all the major senses. Once scent, sound and sight are working in unison, the instinct to survive is switched on. When the response is stimulated, your dog is transformed into a hyper-alert state and ready for action.

STAYING STILL

In some animals, especially the young, passive or non-predatory, the fight or flight response can take on another form known as 'freezing'. This behaviour involves remaining perfectly still in order to avoid the attentions of a predator, a strategy that can be highly effective against fellow canines and feline predators that have comparatively poor vision; both dogs and cats have eyesight evolved to detect movement rather than detail (see page 14). Freeze behaviour is also used by predatory animals to conceal themselves in order to ambush prey. Puppies or cubs in the wild are known to remain still when exposed to a threat or another dog other than their mother.

OVER-EXCITEMENT

Some adult dogs with a hyperactive personality may react to the initial excitement of visitors or an owner returning after absence by urinating when greeting them. This may be a reaction to the fight or flight response, as this causes a hormonal effect on the bladder. The problem can be dealt with by controlling access to threshold hallways and doors with dog gates and by reducing any initial contact and then rewarding subsequent calmer behaviour.

THE LOADED GUN

Once the fight or flight response has been triggered, in his hyper-alert state, your dog is ready to bark and growl at any perceived threat (see pages 138–141). While out walking, your dog's alert levels are naturally higher, and should he be confronted or challenged by another dog, he will be prepared to respond. There is first a 'sensing' or smelling of pheromones which, together with body language and any vocalization (see pages 28–29), will offer instant information about the other dog, including whether the other dog is fearful or confident. In this situation, the fight or flight response is always ready to be triggered. Hopefully, after a sniffing session, both dogs and their owners will happily continue on their way without incident.

Below: Most dogs experience heightened senses of the fight or flight mode – scent, sound and sight – when enjoying the stimulation of a run in the open.

TURBOCHARGING HORMONES

The fight or flight hormones are generated within the adrenal glands situated above the kidneys. Once triggered, these hormones divert the flow of blood from the digestive system and major organs to the skeletal muscles such as the limbs and jaws. If your dog is frightened by a sound or object while on a walk (see pages 126–127), this survival mechanism means that he will be able to run faster, all the way back home if necessary. When confronted by an aggressive animal, the instantaneous fight or flight response will help him to defend himself and fight back. At the same time, stress- and pain-blocking (corticosteroid) hormones are released to prevent him from being hampered in his self-defence by the potential pain of being physically attacked and bitten.

Reading your dog

Body postures

Dogs rely on a mixture of body language and scent signalling to help them communicate with each other. These skills have been developed in order to avoid making social mistakes or incurring an injury. But can you understand your dog's special language?

Flagging intentions

Your dog should already possess these vital social skills or he needs to learn them quickly if his good intentions are to be fully understood by other dogs. Giving out the wrong message can lead to other dogs displaying aggressive behaviour. There are three stages in standard dog body posturing, shown towards people, but also, most importantly, towards other dogs, and should signal current state of mind.

Relaxed The body is flexible, with eyes not fixed ahead but distracted, the head lowered and ears falling loose or softly. The back line is slightly arched or relaxed, with the tail drooping and showing early stages of side-to-side movement before or between the hind legs.

Anticipatory In the second stage, the body is slightly straightened, the head lifted, with eyes checking and ears up, the back stiffened, hindquarters slowly moving and tail up or swinging from side to side. From this position, a playful dog might bow down as an invitation for you or perhaps another dog to join in and play. Vocal dogs will often play bow and play bark too. This is seen as a signal for dogs to begin challenging each other in a playful, non-aggressive way or for you to engage in play.

Readiness In this position your dog is in a state of high alert and can spring into action. The body is more rigid or tense, the eyes fixed and ready for contact, the head held up and forward, the hackles or fur around the shoulder raised, the back line stiffened, the ears up and alert and the tail rigidly held out and back.

Above: The posture of this Dobermann, with the head lifted, ears up and tense back line, suggests that he is trying to anticipate his next move.

Left: The softened posture of this Labrador, with tail low and his back line more fluid, shows that his body is relaxed and he is happy.

Sniffing etiquette

Once your dog has put forward his own personal social strategy by way of his body language, it is usually the turn of the other dog to respond. In the case of contented dogs, this would eventually result in play bowing (see pages 46–47) or an encouragement to race and chase, and even play barking. However, before all this doggy fun can commence, in most instances, both dogs will feel a need to sniff each other and exchange scents.

Carefree, relaxed dogs will often stand and allow their bottoms to be sniffed, and if your dog is likely to do the same, they will stand side by side, heads and tails in opposition. This facilitates the exchange of scents that will confirm the dogs' sex and also the oestrus cycle of a bitch, to find out whether she is ready for mating or not. Scent may also offer information about dominance and a dog's emotional state of mind, such as whether it is fearful or content. Unsolicited sniffing can lead to a warning vocalization or growl (see pages 30–31), or an act of aggression, so it would seem that some dogs wish to withhold scent information.

READING BODY LANGUAGE

The side profile of the three display states, particularly in breeds with a simple body outline, can be plainly read by other dogs. However, the long coats of some breeds can obscure the positioning of the ears and shape of the back line.

Antisocial dogs can fail to learn the states correctly or could even be confused by what should be an instinctive language. A dog wagging his tail from side to side in a friendly fashion can still attack another. This strategy may be used to confuse a competitor or as a precaution by a fearful dog if there is any chance of aggression from another dog. It can be hard to tell, but a contented dog will wag his tail first and ask questions if the other dog does not respond in a similar vein.

Dominant dogs may choose to raise a high tail or a curly tail and still wag it, while others, perhaps sub-dominant, may swing a low tail slowly from side to side and even lie down before offering the underbelly for sniffing. A dominant individual will often stand over the submissive dog, as if to announce his superiority. In the main, body language comes first, occasionally accompanied by basic vocalization such as a play bark. Then, if all is well, comes the sniffing etiquette.

Below: This Boxer is raised to full height and showing a rigid outline that reveals she is ready for action.

Above: The dog bark is basic language for the pack. It alerts both humans and other dogs to potential threats.

Bark, growl and yelp

Your dog has a simple system of vocalizing his intentions and these sounds are used to support his body language. The vocal tones are important to communicate intention and these vary from a low tone to a high-pitched yelp. In the language of dogs, the bark is mainly used as an alert call.

Alert bark

In nature, the wild dog uses a bark – not always repeated – as an alert or warning to other pack members. It usually indicates the presence of other dogs outside the pack, fellow predators or even prey, and is used to bring these to the attention of the other dogs. Once roused, the pack can then come together and operate as a group to deal with the potential threat or meal.

Attention bark

When your dog barks, he is informing you that there is either an unusual noise or a potential threat that needs to be investigated and dealt with accordingly. If you don't deal with it, your dog will take the task upon himself. This may mean

BARKING HABITS

Your dog may have surprised himself when he uttered his first bark. Some dogs have been known to reach sexual maturity before having the confidence to start barking. Others, such as terriers and guarding breeds like the Rottweiler and German Shepherd Dog, seem to enjoy barking, but some become addicted to barking at targets. While it would be easy to believe that this is because they simply enjoy the sound of their own voice, it could be that they become addicted to the apparent success of their barking. Even the Basenji, an African hunting dog that doesn't bark, uses a sound that has been compared to yodelling.

Often the stimulus for barking is an unusual noise or the passing movement of potential targets (threatening or exciting). Barking can also be associated with the sight or sound of other dogs or people passing by or delivering to the home.

displaying hyperactivity, rushing from room to room, hurtling towards the front door or jumping up, all to the tune of the bark. If you instruct him to stop barking and he is properly trained, the barking should cease. He will know that you are dealing with the sound or event or that you consider it not to be a threat.

Play bark

Play barking is a learned response and is your dog demanding attention or to be played with by throwing another ball or frisbee for him to run and catch. Dogs will play bark to each other, and they seem to know the difference between an alert and a play bark, although some that have been poorly socialized may be confused by the two forms of barking. Such play barking means that a dog is excited by the opportunity to play, and it could be compared to children shouting to each other when enjoying a game.

Warning growl

When your dog growls, he could be involved in play fighting (either with you or with another dog) or warning off other dogs before he commits to an attack, signalling to them to back off or risk sustaining injury. Some dogs may use a light play growl when they are interacting with their owners. The tone is not as menacing and can be interpreted as part of the play fighting repertoire.

The canine growl is an instant warning, especially when used among wild dogs. If there is a kill that is not to be shared, a possessive growl will see off another dog hanging

DOGS' VOCAL LANGUAGE

Low tone – play growl; aggressive growl

Middle tone – play bark; alert bark

High tone – submissive or injured yelp; plea whine; separation howl or whine

around for scraps. If there is an *alpha* female being shown attention by a *beta* male, the *alpha* male will growl at him. When there is a hierarchal challenge between males, a warning dominant growl is all that is needed to give the other dog a chance to leave the scene unscathed. The canine growl is very specific to challenge and aggression, which explains why a dog will respond more readily to the deeper, male voice of an owner, heard as a challenge, than to the lighter and higher-toned voice of a female owner.

Below: When dogs play bark or growl, such as during a game of ball, they are using this communication as a practice for when real defence-aggression is necessary.

Submission

Accidentally step on your dog's paws or trap his tail and you will hear a yelp or upper tone. This says that your dog is either slightly hurt or, if repeated, seriously injured. The pitch is one of the highest in dog language, the other being a whine. The yelp is used as a submissive signal in nature where the beaten competitor will show his weakened state to the dominant individual. During play fighting, dogs will yelp in order to be released from a play bite or hold when pinned down.

When dogs whine in order to gain attention from an owner, they are using a plea or submissive behaviour normally associated with early separation from their mother; she may be taking a rest from the puppies or even out hunting in nature. Your dog may use this form of vocalization to encourage you to play or offer food. He will have learned that this passive form of behaviour can sometimes trigger a response from you and may even include a reward in the form of an opportunity to enjoy a walk together. If you are leaving your dog alone at home and he begins to whine repeatedly or if he howls in your absence, this is a sign of over-dependency and problems related to being separated from you (see pages 114–115 and 118–121).

QUESTIONS AND ANSWERS: BARKING

How should I deal with my dog when he won't stop barking when instructed?

When a dog repeatedly barks, he may learn that he can gain extra attention by doing so. The action of excessive barking or whining can be interrupted by using training discs, preassociated with the removal of a food treat (see page 75). Once a dog has stopped barking, a clicker can be used to signal a reward (see page 74). If the repeated barking, or howling or whining, is happening in your absence, this indicates a problem of over-attachment to you as his owner (see pages 114–115 and 118–121).

What should I do if my dog growls at me when we are not playing?

If your dog is growling in a challenging way, first say a firm 'No' or signal clearly with training discs (see page 75). Once the behaviour has been interrupted, say a bright 'Yes' or signal with the clicker (see page 74). In these situations, it is advisable to avoid direct confrontation and eye contact with your dog. The growling or challenging can be over instructions such as 'come down off the furniture' or recall, or over food, giving up a toy or item or removing him from or to another room.

A successful method of changing your dog's behaviour and encouraging him to respond to instructions is to distract him by standing in another room and sounding a whistle, rustling a bag of food or bouncing a ball. Always reward him (verbally or with a food treat, stroke or toy) and say 'Yes' (signal with a clicker, if used) when your dog comes to you and has sat when instructed.

Left: This terrier is showing possessive aggression over a stick found on a walk. To avoid these situations, take toys with you and introduce a food reward when they are retrieved.

Right: Dogs can demand attention, food and play interaction by repeatedly barking. This should be countered at an early stage to prevent it developing into challenging behaviour.

Petting your pet

Your dog just wants to be a part of your social scene, and he approaches you knowing that you are likely to reach down to pat and stroke him. He views this attention from his pack leader positively because he needs leadership reassurance.

WHAT PATTING MEANS

Your dog can use your patting as the first step to gaining more from you. He sniffs and licks your hands, encouraging you to become even more involved. It takes only a glance and tail wag from him for you to switch from patting to stroking to a close cuddle, and maybe it will lead to him being offered a walk or some food.

PUPPY LOVE

Being socially interactive, it doesn't take long for your dog to learn that a 'happy dog' approach, with tail constantly wagging, will earn him lots of attention from family members and friends. Puppies, in particular, crave physical contact from their owners when suffering the after-effects of separation from their mother and siblings, especially prior to sleep periods, because your warmth has the same soothing effect as the closeness that they afforded him.

FORMS OF GROOMING

Your dog happily accepts strokes and even rough physical contact from you because he views this as part of natural grooming behaviour. Try holding his scruff – the loose skin around the back of the neck – and gently rubbing behind the head and under the chin, then tickle his ears. These are very difficult areas for a dog to groom himself. Your willingness to scratch into his scruff (an act that mimics his mother gently biting into the loose skin to carry him) together with any rubbing or tickling is not very different from canine allogrooming or social grooming. In nature, dogs groom each other exclusively through licking as a sign of mutual trust. This is thought to act as a form of appeasement, reducing tension and conflict among groups.

Licking not only has its origins in basic grooming behaviour, but also in tasting and scent recognition, as well as wound cleaning after injury. Repeated licking also produces a calming effect because it triggers the release of 'reward hormones' (see opposite).

IN SUBMISSION

When your dog rolls over and offers his tummy, he is being submissive. The reward of receiving a playful rub from his owner in these situations is more than enough to encourage your dog to repeat this act of submission in order to gain the benefit. In nature, a low-ranking pack member often presents its the vulnerable underbelly and genital regions to a higher ranking member of the pack for sniffing, licking and, in those of a similar status, grooming.

HORMONAL BENEFITS

Your dog also has a chemical reason to enjoy a petting session with you. Grooming behaviour has a soothing effect because it triggers the release of feel-good hormones into your dog's brain. There are three key hormones that are triggered:

Endorphins – blocking stress, pain and irritations

Dopamine – released by the feeling of anticipation triggered by pleasure and soothing contact

Serotonin – released as a specific reward, offering a feel-good factor.

Above: Owners and dogs usually enjoy tactile contact and in these situations stroking has a mutual benefit.

WHAT ARE THE HUMAN BENEFITS TO STROKING A DOG?

When you stroke your dog, it creates a positive effect on your heart's metabolism and triggers the release of the same reward hormones that also help to make your dog content.

Dog ownership has been proven to relax people, reducing their blood pressure and even helping to counter depression. Patients suffering from heart conditions, hypertension, diabetes and many other chronic conditions have shown improvement in health when caring for a dog.

There are schemes in the USA – Animal Assisted Therapy Program – and the UK – Pets as Therapy – that use these benefits by taking dogs into retirement homes, hospices and hospital wards.

Having a dog is good for the head as well as the heart. Psychologists agree that children involved in caring for a dog will improve their IQ as well as increasing their responsibility and respect for animals.

Licking your face

You have returned home from a shopping trip with a friend and there, with an enthusiastic welcome, is your faithful dog. You both kneel down to say 'hello' and your dog begins to lick your faces vigorously. You love your dog but others may find the behaviour a little embarrassing.

Why does he do it?

When your dog attempts to lick your face, he is performing a canine greeting commonly observed in the wild. In nature, juveniles and the potentially *alpha* female that has remained behind to care for her cubs, will enthusiastically greet the returning pack members that have been out hunting. The youngsters and other hungry individuals will jostle with each other and try to lick a hunter-pack member around the neck, throat and mouth as a form of begging. Those returning pack members that have eaten will often use this interaction as a signal to regurgitate partially digested food because they have an innate or genetic response to this submissive behaviour.

So, rather than viewing it from a human perspective as a display of affection by the dog, or even a form of kissing, licking should be seen as a submissive or begging plea, often used to gain access to the owner's attention, perhaps in the hope of triggering an offer of food or the chance of a walk.

What to do

If you think that face licking is undesirable and/or unhygienic, especially with babies and small children, it is important to avoid inadvertently reinforcing the behaviour from an early age by giving your dog attention or physical contact. Instead, reward the puppy for sitting rather than jumping or climbing up on to your knee, and discourage all family members and friends from kneeling or sitting down to the dog's level. If he tries to face lick, turn away without speaking or giving eye contact and, as soon he stops, praise him and give him a quick pat. He will quickly learn that he can gain your attention and physical contact without resorting to licking.

Above left: When a dog licks his owner's face this represents natural submissive behaviour, asking for food or attention.

Right: This Golden Retriever puppy is exhibiting plea behaviour towards the adult dog by licking his mouth.

QUESTIONS AND ANSWERS: LICKING

How can I stop my adult dog from face licking?
As soon as the dog begins to face lick, without using any verbal instruction that could unintentionally give him attention, turn away and avoid physical and eye contact (in difficult situations, introduce a sound like training discs to signal a non-reward, see page 75). Once the dog stops attempting to lick, praise him and offer the chance to play with a toy or sound a clicker as a reward (see page 74).

Is the behaviour detrimental to the dog?
Some insecure dogs become addicted to licking and, in moments of stress such as separation from their owner (see pages 118–121), they will switch to repeated paw or flank licking to trigger the hormone-induced feel-good factor (see page 34). If this behaviour progresses, it could lead to the development of fungal infections and lick granulomas that may require both professional behaviour and veterinary treatment.

Is the behaviour a health risk to humans?
There is a risk to humans in situations where dogs pick up infections after coming into contact with other dogs or animal faeces and then transfer unhealthy bacteria on to owners. In most cases it is a low risk, but one that you should consider when encouraging face-licking behaviour, especially if it involves children.

Licking, scratching and chewing

Certain forms of behaviour come naturally to your dog and they involve his amazing tongue, those fine claws and his healthy set of sharp teeth. These front-end accessories enable him to explore physically all that is on offer in the world around him.

Tongue tool

Your dog will show you his tongue at every opportunity. In hot weather, he needs to pant continually and extend his tongue to distribute saliva that helps cool him down (see page 12). He will lick your hands, face (see pages 36–37) and even your feet, if you let him, through which he obtains scent that confirms the levels of your hormones, health and emotional well-being.

Although not quite as abrasive as sandpaper, the surface of your dog's tongue is rough enough to tease soft food items apart or, as in nature, to pull flesh away from muscles and bones. He can also curl his tongue almost into the shape of a shallow spoon, which allows him to lap liquids up into his throat when drinking.

Clever claws

Your dog has four sets of claws, for scratching under the sofa for his favourite toy just as well as for digging huge holes in the garden. Dogs are naturally burrowing animals and in the wild will use their claws to dig a place to rest and be protected from the worst kinds of weather. You may have seen your dog scratching at the carpet just before he lies down to rest. This equates to making a resting place in the forest or sand more comfortable and free from insects or snakes. Wild dogs will also claw away the skin of prey as they bite into a kill.

In between his claws, which will grow continuously if not worn down through walking or being trimmed, are scent glands that enable him to mark his territory. Dogs that scratch doors and furniture are often exhibiting separation-related disorder in response to being left alone or kept apart from their owner in the home (see pages 122–123).

You may notice your dog using his hind paws and claws to scratch and kick back the ground after he has urinated or defecated. There are several differing views on what this behaviour represents, but marking territory is undoubtedly involved. It may increase the amount of scent that the dog wants to leave, or it could be a strategy to cover up his scent tracks or even to cover up the previous dog's tracks that encouraged him to scent mark in the first place. Some researchers believe it is a deliberate visual or communication display, made in a demonstrative way so that other dogs can observe it. The scratch marks may also act as a visual signal for other dogs.

Talented teeth

Dogs have 42 teeth – more than double the number of a child and ten more than an adult human – made up of seven pairs of premolars, six pairs of molars, six pairs of incisors and two pairs of canines. In wild dogs, the canines and incisors have the task of ripping raw food, while the premolars and molars do the crunching and cracking. Pet food for modern-day dogs may not require such effective flesh-cutting and bone-crushing tools, but our pets still have that capacity and serve to remind us that they are domesticated predators.

A GOOD CHEW

It is a rare dog that doesn't enjoy a good chew. Dogs often relish chewing and licking an uncooked bone or rawhide chew – this repeated action can help to calm a dog by stimulating reward hormones (see page 34). However, care should be taken when offering cooked bones to dogs because they are known to splinter, and sharp or fragmented shards can cause health problems.

Dogs that love to chew shoes and other household items may be bored or suffering from separation-related disorder (see pages 122–123).

Far left: Clearly enjoying himself, this dog is using his combined 'claw and paw' power to dig a potential resting place.

Below: Chewing behaviour comes naturally to all puppies and dogs and has a calming affect on them due to the release of reward hormones.

Natural behaviour

Sleep

Your dog needs to rest in order to charge up his energy batteries, just as you do. The amount of sleep he requires will usually depend on his levels of activity and age. Your dog will seek out the best place for a sleep and knows when to take a nap.

Sleep patterns

Most dogs are happy to share their owners' night-time sleep pattern, but they will also sleep on and off during the daytime when their owners are away from home or otherwise occupied with work or study. Most dogs will, however, adapt to other sleeping schedules if their owners have non-traditional work patterns, providing they are correctly fed and exercised.

DO DOGS DREAM?

During the daytime or early evenings, dogs appear to experience more of a shallow, REM (rapid eye movement) type sleep – a term used to describe the almost conscious period that precedes and follows deep, unconscious sleep. At these times, you may see your dog making running motions even though he is lying down on his side and asleep, and hear him letting out muffled barks.

'Home-alone' dogs often target their owners' beds for sleeping, not simply for comfort but also because the bedroom offers the reassurance of fresh owner scent. Any sleep taken during the daytime will be light and periodic. Some dogs sleep in an alert-ready state, with eyes not fully closed and ears not relaxed. This sleep will be immediately interrupted by routine household sounds, such as post being delivered or the telephone ringing.

Active needs

Active dogs that share extended walks with their owners will, on returning home, eat and then rest. Many working breeds, such as gundogs, sight and scent hounds or livestock-controlling dogs, that are not in active employment are happy to have as many walks as an owner can provide, and will simply sleep after each exercise session to rebuild their energy reserves. This is why mental exercise, such as search and find games with food or toys, can be just as important as physical exercise for healthy dogs. An employed working dog, such as a Border Collie, would have to concentrate and exert much physical energy when racing after strays and rounding up a flock. Without this opportunity, some will sleep extremely sporadically and may even attempt to wake owners up in the early hours. This behaviour can also be linked to problems with separation (see pages 118–121).

Sleep requirements

Puppies are just like babies and need plenty of sleep and rest between periods of activity. When your dog matures from middle to old age, you will notice his energy levels and staying power begin to diminish. Not all elderly dogs are infirm and many owners have reported their older dog gaining renewed vigour, especially when a puppy has joined the family. The younger dog will often tease the older one into joining in his games. Competition will trigger the odd race or two and perhaps a tug-of-war session. The older dog regularly looks for warm places in order to doze, in front of the fireplace or where the sun casts a warm light into a room. You will notice that he takes a longer sleep after a walk, as his body tires more easily.

Above left: These dogs are taking a well-earned rest and replenishing their energy reserves for the next bout of exercise.

Right: With paws extended as if running, this sleeping dog may be dreaming and may even give out muffled woofs.

WHAT IF MY DOG WANTS TO SLEEP AT THE WRONG TIME?

Some dogs will rest throughout the day and most of the evening and then suddenly come to life. This behaviour can be associated with owners who work varying shift patterns or with dogs that are temporarily sleep disorientated because of illness or infirmity. There are also dogs that suffer from noise sensitivity (hyper-alertness), where sudden or unusual noises may keep them awake (see pages 126–127).

The cure can be in recovery or plenty of short, frequently treat-rewarded walks. In some situations with nervous dogs, the solution is to provide them with an indoor crate with a cover or a canvas travel unit to mimic the burrow they would use in nature, in order to make them feel more secure (see pages 120–121). Those dogs that fail to settle at night when separated from their owner might be suffering from separation-related disorder (see pages 118–121).

Grooming

Your dog will require regular grooming. How he views your efforts at keeping him in good condition will depend on his personality. The physical attention you will need to give him and the frequency of grooming will also be determined by his breed and coat type.

Mutual benefits

To your benefit, keeping your dog's skin and coat clean and well groomed will ensure that he looks healthy and sheds fewer hairs. Some dogs clearly enjoy being brushed and combed, particularly those that have been accustomed to regular grooming from puppyhood. Most dogs love to be tickled or stroked in certain places, especially those that they cannot reach to self-groom, such as the dome of the head and back of the neck or under the chin. This obvious enjoyment is probably associated with the memory of their mother's licking and grooming in their very first days.

Seek advice from a breeder or professional dog groomer on how to get the best results from a particular breed's coat. Grooming can be made doubly rewarding for him by offering some food treats for being obedient or calm.

Grooming problems

Some dogs show a distinct dislike of the dog brush or being towelled dry. This situation can arise with dogs that have status problems, such as dominance (see page 64), or rescue dogs that have developed a negative association with being handled, where they perceive the sight of an owner wielding a brush or a towel as a threat. Some dogs can only be groomed by their owner, viewing grooming by others as a form of invasion of their body space.

The potential for some dogs to be sensitive about grooming is because, in terms of dog body language, this action requires mutual trust (see page 34). The insecure or dominant personality might display nervous withdrawal or challenging aggression towards being groomed by skulking or growling. Some dogs may attack or bite the brush.

Above left: Children benefit emotionally from the responsibility of basic dog care and grooming.

Right: Your dog will enjoy you brushing away the tangles around his chin as it represents natural, social grooming.

QUESTIONS AND ANSWERS: GROOMING

How should I react when my dog displays problem behaviour during grooming?
Sound signals, such as the clicker and training discs can be used (see pages 74–75): when your dog is behaving, use the clicker, but if he reacts boisterously or in a challenging way, sound the training discs. In this way, the dog learns that by behaving he will be rewarded.

Is it necessary to groom my dog every day?
A weekly routine of brushing or combing is usually enough for all those except the very long-coated dogs; the latter need a 'little and often' strategy to avoid knots and tangles developing. However, the frequency depends on the kind of walks taken and the coat type.

After a particularly wet walk, the easiest way to dry your dog is with an old bath towel, rubbing to remove dirt and loose hairs. Then follow with a short brushing session. Dogs with especially long-haired coats are much more of a challenge to clean up, so owners need to keep a large stock of towels and be prepared for more lengthy brushing.

Do dogs need baths?
Dogs can be washed with a special dog or baby shampoo every few months or after a particularly wet and muddy expedition, and although your dog may not appreciate the experience, people are likely to stroke him more if he is clean. It is important not to remove too much of the natural skin oils beneath the coat – the top coat or guard hairs are usually tough, but the finer undercoat hairs and skin are more delicate. Washing away these essential oils would leave the dog vulnerable to dermatological conditions.

If you and your dog have enjoyed a trek across farmland with livestock in the vicinity, a towel rubdown is the ideal opportunity to undertake a quick health check and examine his coat for any ticks or signs of fleas.

Play

Dogs express themselves based on a mixture of nature, their breed personality and what they have learned by being around people and other dogs. While he will never let go of his wild side, your dog enjoys the comfort of living with you without having to worry about his chances of survival.

Playing for life

Despite domestication, your dog carries a genetic programme of development. His earliest suckling behaviour, for example, naturally gives way to chewing. But the natural process can be interrupted, as seen in puppies prematurely removed from the litter, which often continue to display suckling beyond this early period but transformed into antisocial mouthing or challenging behaviour (see page 64). Through domestication, dogs have adapted to exhibit a combination of juvenile and adult behaviours throughout their lives – exemplified by their high level of playfulness evident at all ages.

An invitation to play

To elicit your attention, your dog will lower his body and head, wag his tail, lick your hands and rub up against you – the same behaviour he would use to show submission towards older or higher-status dogs in the wild pack, and beg for food that hunting pack members might regurgitate. He will also use his head to nuzzle into you, holding his ears back to offer a passive facial expression. He may even place his paws on your lap to gain attention. Then, if all else fails, he might leave your side and disappear momentarily from the room before returning proudly carrying a toy that he wants to show to you. Just as many dogs play bow towards other dogs in a behaviour that is intended to encourage 'chase or challenge', they also use this to signal towards family members as an invitation to play a game. However, rather than give in on demand, it is advisable for owners to announce play sessions rather than allow the dog to believe he is in charge of them.

Above: *Dogs may be reluctant to give up a toy but encourage them by always rewarding with verbal praise and an occasional treat when they do.*

WHY DOESN'T MY DOG WANT TO PLAY?

There are a number of reasons why a dog might show a lack of interest in playing retrieval games. There are many gundog breeds that retrieve by instinct, but if a dominant or possessive individual is challenging his owner, returning and giving back a ball or frisbee would be, in dog body language, a sign of submission. These dogs might return the item to their owner, but often not give it up or deliberately drop it elsewhere. There are also many breeds with skills and personalities that are out of tune with the run and fetch task. However, with the encouragement of food rewards, most dogs will play and retrieve.

Some dogs may not have learned how to play or may have developed negative associations with play, through children or adults being too rough, or through poor or interrupted socialization at the litter stage. Some old or overweight dogs may find even the idea of play too exhausting.

Point-scoring games

Sometimes a toy carried by your dog will trigger a tug-of-war game – he won't let go until the last moment, when he realizes that you are much stronger than him. On other occasions, your dog will show you the toy or even an item that belongs to you and then run off with it in the hope that you will chase after him. This 'chase and race' behaviour is a physical challenge, a test to find out who is the fastest, strongest or fittest. These point-scoring games are a method of gathering knowledge about the 'competition'. In nature, this type of information provides useful potential ranking information among maturing pack members.

Problem play

Happy and contented dogs instinctively know when interactive play with an owner is appropriate, and also sense the difference between play biting and aggression. However, there are some, often terriers or fighting breeds, that rapidly become highly aroused and may develop hyperactive and aggressive behaviours when playing on the floor with owners or once they are outdoors, which can turn play sessions into antisocial events. You can provoke these problems by playing too much tug-of-war with your dog or inadvertently encouraging his hyperactivity by rewarding the behaviour with direct attention. You need to dictate the play rules to your dog, so that he will know when, where and how the interaction is appropriate. In this way your dog will *sense* that you are pack leader.

Above: *The play bow is commonly displayed by companion dogs and is an invitation for owners and dogs to interact.*

Below: *A frisbee is an ideal toy to take on walks to help introduce brief retrieval sessions with your dog.*

Dogs form varying degrees of attachment to their owners and immediate family. This is exactly in keeping with how they would develop socially with their mother, siblings and pack members in nature. How healthy and successful your dog's relationship is with you is influenced by his personality, breed and early experiences.

Relationships and attachments

FAMILY ROLES

If a puppy's new home includes an adult female, she will quickly become his replacement mother, the sex of whom he will have established through detecting hormone levels, such as oestrogen. Adult female dog owners are naturally maternal in their early relationship with a young dog, and therefore their choice as replacement mother is a functional one. She would be recognized by a dog as the *alpha* female in the home. A male owner will most likely be viewed as the *alpha* male or lead protector of the human-canine pack. Children, with their usually lower levels of hormones, are most likely to be regarded as fellow puppies or cubs. The puppy forms his early relationships based on these factors.

As dogs reach sexual maturity, unless they are neutered (see pages 68–71), their needs change in subtle ways. Owners can become potential mates if opposite sexes are matched, and although these relationships are unfulfilled in the biological sense, they can increase the degree of attachment that a dog forms.

PERSONALITY AND BREED FACTORS

A dog's daily requirement of interaction with his owner depends on his personality and if there is any 'working'

aspect in his breeding, which brings with it a demand for higher levels of activity and interest, with only brief interludes for resting and feeding to recharge energies. Some owners thrive on active or extrovert canines, viewing them as entertaining or characterful companions, while others may find such demands for constant activity or a hyperactive personality too exhausting.

In complete contrast to the active or extrovert personalities, there are those dogs that form a relationship with one person. Other family members and friends are only given attention in terms of superficial greetings or in order to obtain food. There is always a danger that this 'bonding' can become too vital for the dog and that eventually he cannot bear to be apart from his owner (see pages 114–115 and 118–121). Some owners desire this significant level of attachment in their dogs, while others view the dog's consequent stress due to separation as a problem personality trait. It all depends on what you expect of your dog. A dog's expectations are, on the other hand, more straightforward. They live in the 'now' and, although they can anticipate when owners are returning home because of work or study patterns, they accept separation as part of normal life cycles.

Above: Young dogs develop attachments to owners that suggest unconditional love and loyalty and will accept as much owner attention as they can get. However, this can lead to problem attachments on both sides.

DEMANDING VERSUS BONDING

Demanding dogs find it quite easy to burn up all the attention any family member or friend may choose to offer and they can still be looking for more. They will often seek out the weakest link in a family group and naturally exploit this weakness or kindness to gain the necessary attention. Variously described as 'bold', 'alert', 'lively', 'energetic' and 'outgoing', the more interaction these dogs receive, the more they will need. Such dogs will appear tireless, especially in their relentless quest for human interaction.

Terms such as 'one-man dog', 'biddable', 'faithful' and 'loyal' tell something of the story about the special bond some dogs can form with owners. These strong attachments are often found in individuals from the true working breeds, such as the Border Collie, but not always so. Many lap dogs or small to medium companion breeds can show the same powerful bonding traits towards willing owners.

Curiosity

Young dogs have a huge amount of curiosity, and any new environment or situation interests all but the most timid of dogs. Your dog's world is a playground teeming with excitement and the occasional reason to be a little apprehensive. Try looking at the world from his viewpoint in order to understand his perspectives.

Above: *A curious dog will follow you to ascertain what is going on around him as he tries to find a place in the human–canine pack.*

Exploring his environment

It isn't just cats that are blessed with a natural sense of curiosity. Your dog will have undoubtedly shown the curious side of his personality from the moment he first started to explore your home.

There are two distinct worlds to the explorer dog:
1 Home, where he and his pack members (you and your family) live.
2 The world outside, full of interesting things; some promising, others threatening.

These spheres will usually have opened up to him in stages. Most dogs are kept indoors prior to completing the necessary vaccination programme. Once he has explored every room in the home, house-training will give him access to the immediate vicinity. As he begins to walk the neighbourhood with you, he will explore everything that is new, including every tree or lamp post and all the freshly produced scents of other dogs and animals. Your dog will employ all his senses, but the most powerful trigger for his exploratory instinct is usually associated with scent. Once smelt, seen and heard, finally he may lick or chew the target of his curiosity.

Checking out other animals

When exposed to a newly introduced kitten, your dog may either approach it enthusiastically or with caution, sometimes even moving slowly forwards on his belly – the behaviour he performs will be based on his prior knowledge. If he is familiar with cats, he may ignore it out of lack of interest.

Alternatively, he could display a friendly or aggressive reaction depending on his previous experiences. He may bark or growl at the kitten to see how it reacts or he might start to lick its fur in an attempt to groom and bond with his newfound friend.

Dogs will naturally feel the need to check out all other animals unless they are fearful or have had a difficult experience and subsequently formed a negative association. They may chase after a pet rabbit or banish birds feeding on the lawn. Worst still, they may try to chase livestock and appear extremely enthusiastic when sheep or cows run away. Although these behaviours are instinctive in dogs, they are obviously undesirable and should be dealt with carefully (see pages 140–141).

Investigating other dogs

Your dog will want to investigate any other dog he comes into contact with. Dogs are social animals in every sense of the term and, after performing all the necessary body and scenting moves (see pages 28–29), they will sniff and be sniffed. However, not all other dogs want to be sociable and it is sometimes prudent to ascertain from the owner the sociability of an approaching dog to avoid any social mishaps. When your dog is off-lead, however, it is not always possible to check on the credentials of other dogs. Even the

most sociable of dogs can develop problem behaviours
if they are attacked by another, antisocially behaved dog.
Some doggy victims develop a 'get in first' strategy after
being attacked, and this can make walks less pleasurable
for all concerned. It is advisable to use a 'reward whistle'
to motivate your dog to return if he might be exposed
to an aggressive dog (see page 75). The whistle should be
used first around the home so that it is not associated with
meeting other dogs outdoors. Then it can be used to motivate
recall in difficult circumstances.

*Below: This spaniel is displaying a natural
curiosity and is enjoying checking out
the unusual scents and novel behaviour
of pond life.*

HIDDEN DANGERS

Some cupboards in your home may house some
potentially dangerous items. A young dog may explore
plastic bottles and containers in moments of boredom by
licking and chewing them, so it is important either to
install childproof catches or store any such items out of
his reach. Dogs need to be kept away from any chemical
spillage because they can easily walk through it and then
lick and groom themselves, thus ingesting the toxic
substance. If in doubt, after a walk or following a home
spillage, wash your dog's pads in a bowl of lukewarm
soapy water.

Male and female attitudes

Dogs of both sexes share most behavioural traits, but there are a few subtle differences that set them distinctly apart. If dogs are from Pluto, then bitches are from Saturn.

Sex and personality

A male and female dog can possess a similar personality. While female dogs are widely accepted to be more docile than male dogs and display less-challenging behaviour, this view may fall down when a placid male is directly compared to a dominant female. Similarly, many people believe that bitches are more faithful or biddable than their male counterparts, but there are a great many male dogs that show these same characteristics. Again, it depends on the individual personality, and breed type has a huge influence. The view that male dogs are more aggressive than bitches is not strictly correct, according to animal behaviour clinic statistics. Male dogs do have a tendency to be more competitive and as such may challenge each other more. But clinic treatment figures for neutered dogs show that they are just as likely to display antisocial behaviour as entire dogs, although neutered dogs are less likely to wander. There is a natural female maternal instinct that in principle encourages a bitch to show natural caring behaviour. This makes a female dog more endearing for some owners. Male dogs can display an independent air, but this is not an exclusively male personality trait.

Sexual differences

There is a high percentage of behaviour, linked to hormones and controlled in the brain, that is shared between dogs and bitches. However, when it comes to sexual attraction, there are definite behavioural differences between the two sexes. Entire dogs – males that have not been castrated – can pick up the scent of an available bitch – 'on heat' or 'in season' – from hundreds of metres or yards away. Males possess a sexual drive so strong in some cases that it can cause them to break out of their home or garden to get to a female in season. This urge to seek out bitches is very much a male behaviour, although some female dogs have been observed showing a strong interest in males in the vicinity.

NEUTERING EFFECTS

As well as quelling a male dog's urge to roam, neutering will also eliminate inappropriate mounting or displaced sexual behaviour, where a dog will attempt to mount a person's leg or cushions or toys. This behaviour is often triggered by a hormonal surge in the period prior to them reaching sexual maturity and can be reinforced through owner attention or punishment (see pages 70–71). However, the behaviour is also, although less commonly, observed in bitches and in this situation can be a sign of a female challenging the status of her owner. The castrated male remains male orientated in his brain, just as the spayed bitch remains female orientated, and any natural gender influence in personality will continue for the lifetime of the dog.

Physical factor

When dogs and bitches have reached sexual maturity, there is one obvious visual difference in behaviour between them in that the male will 'cock' or lift his leg to urinate, while the female squats. As puppies, both sexes perform the same squatting behaviour when urinating and some late-developing males may continue to do so long after most others have learned to aim higher, the object being to leave a mark just a little above that of a competitor. Perhaps this behaviour is intended to encourage other dogs into believing that the previous high-urine mark was made by a really huge male and that his territory is best avoided. An alternative theory is that females walking along and casually sniffing at a convenient head height would be encouraged to seek out this top dog. Whatever the true reason, your male dog lifts his leg instinctively.

Far left: This male and female pair appear at ease. Dogs socialize with each other in different ways and any initial interactive behaviour is influenced by gender.

Below: These dogs are using their incredible sense of smell to obtain important information about each other, including gender.

Puppyhood

Weaning

The earliest behavioural developments in puppies are entirely instinctive. To survive, they must locate the nearest available teat and begin sucking. This innate response, following birth and contact with their mother, is natural to all mammals. But for them to continue developing, puppies need to be weaned from their mother's milk on to solid food.

From suckling to lapping

Suckling and mouthing are probably the most instinctive behaviours that a puppy will display from the outset. Once the mother has groomed or cleaned her newly birthed puppy, he will naturally make the short journey to her teats without being able to see or hear what is going on around him. The mother may actively encourage him to find his place in these early moments of what is known in puppy development as the reflex period. Sometimes she will even pick him up in her gentle, maternal mouth rather than let him blindly struggle.

For puppies to begin putting on significant weight, they need to be weaned off their mother's milk – their necessary diet during the first three or four weeks – on to a combination of wet foods and prepared milk. To facilitate this important change in diet, the puppy naturally progresses from suckling to lapping.

Nature's way

In nature, the litter-mother would offer her youngsters, who can see and hear from the age of two to three weeks, regurgitated solid food, once she was free from intensive caring to eat for herself. These meals would be partially broken down and fully masticated into a soup-like food.

Above: Puppies instinctively locate the litter-mother's source of milk and will suckle many times throughout the day and night.

Left: A puppy soon learns how to lap up liquids and can then quickly move on to semi-solid foods.

The transfer of enzymes and bacteria from her digestive system and saliva are absorbed by the regurgitated food and probably help the puppies adapt more easily to the necessary dietary change from milk to solids. This interaction would also counter and stabilize their continual feeding demands. In the home situation, the breeder and then you as the subsequent owner replicate these changes and trigger the change from lapping to chewing by first feeding easily digested wet foods and milk and then by introducing semi-solid puppy food.

Learning to chew

Once puppies begin to eat more solid foods on a regular basis, from six to eight weeks old, they quickly learn to chew. There is often a crossover period in feeding behaviours and some puppies can annoy their mothers by switching too early from suckling to chewing. Normally, the breeder will have already started encouraging the natural developmental changes in feeding behaviour, and by the time he has reached your home, your puppy should be able to lap moist foods and milk enthusiastically.

When a puppy begins to chew his food, he will then be able to receive all the necessary balance of proteins, essential fatty acids, carbohydrates, fibre and vitamins and minerals to fuel his juvenile to adult growth. His chewing abilities become increasingly stronger as his milk teeth give way to the larger and much stronger adult teeth (see page 61).

WHAT IF MY PUPPY SHOWS A LACK OF INTEREST IN HIS FOOD?

Breeders will provide a diet sheet for a puppy to enable you to continue to offer him the foods that he is used to. Food variation, if offered in the early stages, can often stimulate enthusiasm. Always exercise or play with your puppy before offering him food. This will trigger his natural need to refuel and encourages him to rest and digest his food afterwards.

Below: *From six to eight weeks old, puppies can bite and chew more solid foods, and your puppy will look forward to his mealtimes.*

Early behaviours

Puppies are filled with equal amounts of energy and curiosity, and some of their earliest behaviours are linked to these two triggers. Like children, puppies obviously need to eat and sleep, but then they want to test out their physical strength by climbing, pulling, running and exploring a world that is ever-expanding at this stage.

His view of you

Your own sex will partially dictate how a young puppy views you. If you are a female owner, he will most likely accept you initially as a replacement for his mother. In the absence of her and his siblings, a puppy will need to take comfort in the form of being given food by you. He will gain warmth from your closeness and cuddles, but what he really needs is your guidance. His instinct is to explore the ever-widening world, but for him to do that confidently, he needs to be encouraged or shown the way. If you are a male owner, he will probably look to you for leadership, but once he reaches sexual maturity between 9 and 12 months of age, he will either defer to you as the natural 'top dog' or begin to challenge you as a male rival (see pages 64–65).

First explorations

Prior to having his final vaccinations, when a puppy can be allowed to explore the outside world, he normally remains in the home, so this is his adventure playground. His nest or 'den' is his basket or indoor crate/kennel, and it is from here that he will make his initial forays into your home. A puppy can use his powerful sniffing abilities and his acute hearing to sense what is going on around him. His eyes detect your movements, rather than contrast and detail, so your passing feet or welcoming arms will probably attract his playfulness. Everything is at ground level for a young dog, unless you pick him up or have him lying in your lap. A puppy starts by exploring his first room and builds up a mental map of it, and then the adjacent rooms as he gains access. Some areas in your home, such as stairs or steps, can present a real physical challenge to a small dog and they will only be comfortably negotiated when his confidence and size allows.

Puppy greetings

When a puppy first sees you, if he is wide awake, he will bound towards you in a happy, juvenile way. His body language – body wiggling and tail wagging – tells you that he is excited and pleased to see you. Teaching a puppy to sit and be calm rather than jumping up when first greeting visitors or family members means he will not become a nuisance as an adult dog.

Sometimes his excitement triggers the passing of a small amount of urine that a confident adult dog would reserve for scent marking. This behaviour is caused by a mixture of pure pleasure and submissiveness. Most puppies grow out of it, but there are cases where the problem can develop in mature dogs. The key to dealing with the behaviour in an adult dog is to reduce the initial hyperactivity and only to reward calmness (see pages 124–125).

HOW WILL I KNOW WHEN MY PUPPY WANTS TO TOILET?

You can usually approximately calculate when a puppy wants to urinate or defecate, that is, immediately before or after food and following a sleep or rest period. It is also possible to read the warning signs – he will begin to sniff and explore with just a little more energy than is expected and may try to sneak under an item of furniture. If you catch your puppy just prior to him squatting, you can gently transfer him outdoors or on to newspapers or a nappy-like puppy pad kept by the door to the outside. Giving lots of praise when he uses this site will encourage him to use it again.

Some owners find that introducing a clicker-reward system (see page 74), even at this early stage, can make house-training swift and successful. This approach will enable you to encourage toileting on demand later in life, which is useful when your dog is in public places and you want to control where and when he urinates or defecates.

Far left: Like children, puppies need to play, eat and sleep in regular cycles, as well as interact with their family 'pack'.

Below: A young dog, brimming with health and vitality, will greet owners with abundant enthusiasm.

Physical and sensory development

Puppies tend to mature very quickly. One minute your new dog can be comfortably picked up with one hand, but in the next, except the toy and miniature breeds, he will appear to have suddenly outgrown your outspread arms. He needs to develop fast – in nature, his survival would have depended upon it.

Body

The growth rate of a puppy is fast, but it varies according to breed. Large, weighty and long-legged breeds often appear quite gangly for the first six months. Small breeds tend to develop physically more slowly than large dogs and are often the most long-lived. Large breeds that are naturally athletic or energetic may experience distinctive growth spurts in muscles and bones. Consequently, it is important not to encourage hyperactivity, as muscle and bone injuries can be caused by over-strenuous play sessions.

Male puppies when urinating usually continue to squat in the same manner as bitches, but once the testicles drop and the necessary hormonal changes occur at the onset of sexual maturity (9 to 12 months of age), they will begin to lift a leg. Females will usually come into season for the first time during this period, with two weeks of light bleeding or a slight swelling of the vulva often being the only initial indication. Some young bitches become broody at this stage and will take toys into the basket and repeatedly groom them.

HOW CAN I STOP MY PUPPY FROM CHEWING THE WRONG THINGS?

First, offer him healthy targets on which he can direct his desire to chew. These can be food sticks, chews or toys designed for dogs to chew. If you catch your puppy chewing a household object, redirect his behaviour to the appropriate item and praise him or use training discs to signal non-reward (see page 75). Once you have interrupted his behaviour, it is important to offer an appropriate replacement for him to channel his chewing needs.

Above: *This young, alert puppy still has his soft coat which will become rougher as he reaches physical maturity.*

Right: *Chewing helps a puppy to exchange milk teeth for more powerful adult teeth. Always provide an appropriate item such as a hide chew or raw bone.*

Coat

Between 12 and 24 weeks of age, the soft, almost downy puppy coat is replaced by tougher surface hairs. When you are stroking or playing with a puppy, the gradual changes in the texture and thickness of his fur will become more noticeable. If a stranger comes into your home, you might see his coat standing up and a line of thick fur around the neck. Depending on his confidence, you may also see his back and tail lift up. This is the early development of body language linked to social behaviour (see pages 28–29) that helps him find his place and role within family life.

Teeth

A puppy's prickly sharp milk teeth emerge just after he finishes suckling and starts lapping up wet or semi-solid foods. He can begin shedding these from around 12 weeks of age, with all of them normally being replaced by adult teeth, in a gradual process, by 18 to 24 weeks old. Until the milk teeth are lost, a puppy will endlessly chew, but this natural behaviour can be directed towards healthy food items and specially designed toys. In most cases, juvenile chewing abates once the adult teeth are in place, but some young dogs continue repetitive biting until they form a destructive obsession (see pages 148–149). If the targets of this destructive behaviour are household items, this can be related to canine stress (see pages 122–123).

Above: A puppy will soon recognize the sounds of his bowl being filled and placed on the floor, stimulating his natural curiosity and learning processes.

Senses

A puppy will learn about daily life in the family home through cues. He will listen for the sound of approaching footsteps. His hearing will become attuned to the sound of the doorbell, your car and the rustling of food packets or the stirring of a spoon in his food bowl. He will react to the smell of food at feeding times and will stand or sit by your side in anticipation. Once he has been fully vaccinated and can explore outdoors, he will show a strong desire to sniff every blade of grass or object that has been scented or marked by other dogs or animals. He will learn to associate your actions with certain activities, for example, changing your shoes and putting on a coat as the signal for a walk. If certain pre-walk associations cause a dog to become over-enthusiastic it can be useful to put the 'cues', such as keys, leads, coats and shoes, in a different room so that they can be calmly and quickly brought into view.

Puppies develop both physically and emotionally in stages. They start life totally dependent on their mother's nurturing care, but just a month or two later, they begin to test their strength and sensory skills against siblings and humans. Within six months, most breeds are equipped to explore and challenge the world around them.

A

B

C

D

Growth development

NEWBORN (**A**)

Puppies are born with sight or hearing not yet fully developed (the reflex period), and so are entirely dependent on their mother for nutrition and care. She grooms the youngsters to prevent them from being vulnerable to diseases, which then stimulates them to toilet. She also cleans up this by-product of her milk.

2–3 WEEKS (**B**)

The mother begins to guide her puppies to urinate and defecate unaided outside the nesting or sleeping area. The fast-developing puppies can now hear and smell, and begin to grow teeth ready for eating regurgitated foods in nature or semi-moist foods in domestication. People known to the mother can start to handle the puppies carefully, to promote early human socialization. The puppies are still not confident on their legs, but their strength is increasing by the day.

4–5 WEEKS (**C**)

The puppies can now walk with some confidence and see more clearly as they enjoy the stimulation of increasingly exploring the world around them. The mother continues to offer milk, warmth and comfort, and will gently but firmly discipline her offspring, especially when their play biting and mouthing becomes too demanding. She will return any wandering individuals to the group if any explore too far too soon, and keep the whole litter under her watchful supervision until she feels that they are strong enough to be allowed their independence.

E   F   G   H

6–8 WEEKS (D)

The puppies' senses and physical strengths are in full working order. Keen to explore away from their mother, they are establishing full independence. She is likely to be grateful for these interludes alone that allow her to rest and recover from giving birth and caring for her youngsters. Siblings are constantly challenging each other in an early prelude to establishing a sense of pack structure and hierarchy. With a full set of pin-sharp milk teeth, all the puppies are now happy to eat more solid foods. Most are ready for their first vaccinations.

9–11 WEEKS (E)

Most puppies will be enjoying life with their new owners, having been fully weaned off liquid or semi-moist food. They will have undergone their second vaccinations and can explore the outside world, during which they will employ all their physical energy in sniffing, licking, chewing, jumping and running, followed by resting. All should be fully house-trained and ready for obedience training.

JUVENILE (F) (12 WEEKS–6 MONTHS)

At this stage, a dog should be completely socialized into his new family. He should be biddable and obedient, and understand that his place is at the bottom of the human–canine pack. Any early problem behaviour, such as play biting and jumping up, should be countered before it becomes a habit (see page 75).

ADOLESCENT (G) (6–18 MONTHS)

Males will begin to lift a leg when urinating with the onset of sexual maturity, around 9–12 months of age, and females will usually come into season for the first time (see page 60). Some dogs with a developing tendency towards dominance and increasing testosterone levels may feel confident enough to challenge their owners. Any antisocial behaviour, such as growling over food or toys, should be dealt with carefully (see pages 64–65).

ADULT (H) (18 MONTHS AND OVER)

A dog's personality is now fully formed. All his breed-specific physical influences will have combined with hormonal changes and social interaction to prepare him for the rest of his life. Despite the adage that you can't teach an old dog new tricks, problem behaviour can still be corrected, but the older the dog, the longer it will take to change (see pages 112–141). Most dogs stabilize at their final average weight and size by the age of three.

Testing and challenging behaviours

Although play should be an important part of a dog's day, it is essential that you control how a play session begins and develops. It is also important that you don't allow your puppy to become possessive over his toys.

Test of strength

When a puppy brings a toy or other item to you and then drops it at your feet or on to your lap, he is demanding to be played with but only on his terms. The favourite game of a challenging puppy is testing his pulling and biting strength against your holding strength, and the easiest way for him to do this is through games of tug-of-war. Although at this stage you will be strong enough to win most bouts, his strength will increase with growth and one day he might be able to win. He will show the toy to you and then turn his head away as an invitation to his test-of-strength game. When an owner lets go of a pull toy in a game, either through deliberate release or as an accidental act, a challenging puppy taking the item away will probably believe that he has won the encounter. He might then increase the frequency of tests because his confidence grows from succeeding.

Challenging leadership

If you throw a ball to be retrieved by a challenging puppy, he will most likely run after it, but once picked up, he may not want to give it back or he might drop it away from you. In this way, he is challenging your leadership. If he growls or behaves possessively over toys or food, he is displaying competitiveness. Other signs of a desire to compete are seeking vantage points such as lying on top of the stairs or jumping on to the sofa to be on the same level as you. He will also want to push through doorways and gateways ahead of you. This is known as dominance or status seeking and needs to be dealt with correctly.

Other problem signs

Sometimes challenging behaviour in puppies can be seen in other more subtle ways, such as through persistent signs of disobedience or a refusal to respond on walks or in vehicles. One distinct sign is when a puppy only selectively responds to recall. Problem behaviours often occur when adrenaline levels (influencing excitement, arousal and awareness) are at their highest. This is usually prior to or during walks and when visitors arrive or depart.

QUESTIONS AND ANSWERS: CHALLENGING

Why does challenging start in some puppies but not others?
Research suggests that the seeds are sown at the litter stage. Any health problems, mistakes in rearing or neglect that occur in the first eight weeks, in relation to humans, the mother, siblings or other dogs, can trigger antisocial behaviour in a young dog.

How can I deal with challenging behaviour?
If he won't respond to an instruction or willingly give up an item, introduce a squeaking toy or blow a whistle away from the incident. Then call your dog to you and reward his obedience with a pat, or 'click and treat' him (see page 74) for giving up the item or for responding to the recall and sit instruction. After a play session, if there is a toy he wants to challenge you over and he is growling, use the sound signal in another room (or training discs, see page 75) when you wish to remove it. Once distracted, leave him in the room, collect the toy and keep it away from him and under your control.

How can I make sure that my dog knows I am his 'pack leader'?
Offer him attention on your terms rather than the other way round, which includes you going through doorways first and eating first. Even if you are not ready for a meal, pretend to eat some of his food in front of your puppy before feeding him. Discourage him from sitting or lying on furniture with you, where he might attempt to elevate his status over yours. If your puppy pulls on walks, instruct him to stop and sit before proceeding. He will soon learn that pulling means 'stop' but behaving means 'going forwards'.

Far left: *Dogs enjoy being able to 'test' out their owners by using their own strength in tug-of-war games.*

Left: *Even miniature dog breeds can challenge an owner by holding on to a ball and refusing to give it back.*

Stealing

A puppy will instinctively attempt to exploit moments of chaos, such as unexpected visitors arriving at your home, and any weakness shown by you, your family and friends. This behaviour is not motivated by nastiness, in human terms. Your dog is simply trying to get what he wants and will make full use of any means that come his way.

Foraging opportunities and targets

Foraging or 'finding and carrying off' behaviour is quite natural in dogs and in many gundog breeds it has been actively selected as a desirable trait. Puppies don't know where, how, why or when exciting opportunities will occur, but they are usually clever enough, in an instinctive sense, to make use of them when they do.

Your dog's main targets for displaced foraging or stealing will be unattended food items in the kitchen or living room. But targets can also be non-edible items, with the 'top ten' being trainers, shoes, slippers, underwear, socks, towels, handkerchiefs, tissues, mobile phones and remote controls. These household items all have one aspect in common: by handling or wearing them, you are marking them every day with your body scent. Your dog will run off with his chosen object and may even show it to you in some instances in the hope that you will chase after him.

Reaping the rewards

In these situations, a puppy is not unlike a naughty child, and he may even seek attention or misbehave simply in order to get a reaction from you or your guests. On occasions, your puppy may trigger a drama and sometimes he may frustrate or even anger you. This makes his game even more successful. Some puppies naturally test owners in order to establish their ranking within the human–canine pack.

Above left: *Dogs enjoy 'stealing' items of clothing, such as shoes, that their owners have scented as the smell represents a connection with the human pack member.*

Right: *Many working breed dogs enjoy retrieving owner items but it is important not to reward this behaviour with attention.*

QUESTIONS AND ANSWERS: ATTENTION-SEEKING FORAGING

How do I deal with my puppy's stealing?
It is important not to make his behaviour into a game by chasing after him or demanding the return of the item, because this again would signify you joining in his game. Always say 'No' or, better still, sound training discs that have already been associated with the removal of a food treat to signal to him that you are not pleased with his behaviour (see page 75). Then use a sound signal, such as a whistle, linked to reward and offer a special food treat to him when your puppy comes to you (see page 75). The offer of a chance to play as a distraction, such as bouncing a ball or sounding a squeaking a toy in another room, will usually encourage a fast response. To reinforce the message, deliberately place an inappropriate item in his view, and as he goes to take it, use the sound of training discs to prompt him to associate this behaviour with a sound that he does not enjoy. On the positive side, you can harness his natural foraging skills with games that involve hidden toys and food treats.

Should he know that I am angry with him?
It is very important that you don't allow his natural behaviour to frustrate or anger you. Bear in mind that you can easily psychologically alter his mind set by distracting him and turn the situation into one that you can control. The best method is to sound training discs (see page 75) and then use a 'reward whistle' (see page 75), or to bring out the dog lead or rustle a food bag. If these actions are used casually rather than directly at the puppy, he will willingly come to you, because he wants to interact.

Neutering

There was once a movement among veterinarians that favoured neutering dogs at a young age on health grounds, but now many older dogs are also neutered when they have behavioural problems. The overall effects of this surgery are not always obvious and the operation can even lead to further complications.

Effects on males and females

The average age for a male dog to be castrated is six months, whereas a female dog may be neutered or spayed following her first season. Neutering a male dog is not a complicated surgical procedure for a trained veterinary surgeon. The operation is far more complex for a female dog, especially if it involves removal of all the reproductive organs such as the ovaries, fallopian tubes and the uterus.

The effects of neutering on a male dog are usually straightforward. As his testosterone levels decrease, he will stop wanting to wander off to seek out females, which can otherwise become a major issue, as a male dog can smell the scent of a bitch in season from considerable distances away, even up to several miles if the wind is blowing in the right direction. Any inappropriate mounting will stop altogether (see pages 70–71).

The neutering of bitches usually eliminates displaced nesting behaviour, where a female will begin scratching in the corners of the home, then seeking out or calling to males when a natural hormonal change brings on the oestrus cycle and she is ready for mating, as well as maternal aggression – a form of protective behaviour.

Left: *Young dogs, when neutered at around six months of age, are effected less than when surgery is performed on an older dog.*

Right: *These puppies are showing signs of developing aggression which is rarely reduced by neutering, however it does prevent wandering in search of a mate.*

QUESTIONS AND ANSWERS: NEUTERING

Will neutering stop my dog being aggressive?

The mechanism of aggression and the 'flight or fight response' is reliant on adrenaline (see pages 24–25), but although neutering is often the first option for treating aggression or dominance in male dogs, it does not appear to reduce the levels of adrenaline in a dog's brain. Neutered male dogs will continue to display a range of aggressive behaviours, from possessiveness to dog on dog (intraspecific) aggression. A similar hormonal situation occurs in bitches, where fear-based aggressive behaviour is believed to be triggered by higher levels of oestrogen and testosterone at the point of sexual maturity (6–12 months of age). Again, neutered female dogs continue to display fear-based and inter-bitch aggression despite having had the surgery.

Are there health and practical reasons for neutering?

There are a number of reasons, mainly based on health grounds, for neutering dogs. Life expectancy is said to increase, with the downside being potential weight gain and a natural reduction in energy drive. Some male dogs develop a condition where the testicles fail to descend, and surgery ensures that there are no complications in what would otherwise be a natural physical development in male dogs. There is an argument for neutering male and female dogs as a way of reducing the risk of cancer-related conditions that are linked to the sexual reproductive organs and mammary glands.

For owners of dogs of both sexes, neutering can be a practical way to ensure that any accidental matings are avoided. Neutered bitches rarely display displaced nesting behaviour (see above) and the maternal drive linked to changing hormone levels is completely countered by the surgery.

Is it advisable to allow a bitch to have puppies before she is neutered?

There are no physical or psychological health reasons why a bitch should reproduce and have puppies. Many contented female dogs have not been mated and allowed to produce a litter of puppies.

Displaced sexual behaviour

When dogs behave in a sexual manner towards an inappropriate target, the myth is that it is simply about frustration. A common reaction is for a dog to be allowed to mate once or a bitch to have one litter as a solution to the problem. However, in reality, there are millions of dogs that don't display problem sexual behaviour and most of them won't have fulfilled the canine mating process.

Dogs of both sexes can develop inappropriate mounting or displaced sexual behaviour as they reach sexual maturity. When visitors first arrive at a home, there is often a period of activity and heightened sense of excitement when people greet each other, including lots of physical contact and body language such as hugging, kissing and shaking hands. In the midst of all this human activity, the dog may naturally become excited.

Hormonal surges

There is a complex combination of influences and a number of triggers for this specific type of innate or genetically influenced behaviour. The first of the known influences is the natural surge of the hormones testosterone and oestrogen that occurs in both sexes of all breeds as they reach sexual maturity. The actual timing of a dog reaching a sexually mature age varies from breed to breed – some smaller breeds attain maturity as early as seven months, while larger breeds often have longer maturing periods of up to 12 months.

Some individual dogs may experience an unusual surge in these hormones at an early stage in their physical development that could trigger a reflex (automatic) behaviour leading to mating or 'mounting'. In the absence of another dog to 'practise' or mate with, an owner or visitor (who is considered to be part of the human–canine pack) may offer an outlet for normal sexual development. Since there are fundamental physical differences between humans and dogs, most obviously height, a human leg is probably the only practical access for the dog's behaviour.

Above: Even young dogs such as this puppy may display inappropriate mounting behaviour as they begin to sexually mature.

CHALLENGING CASES

The problem of displaced sexual behaviour in dogs can also be seen in cases of a female owner with a male dog or a dominant bitch that is challenging their leadership. Where a female is displaying this behaviour, the dog is often continually challenging the owner over access to toys and food and in physically positioning herself, for example, on the sofa, stairs or floor space.

Over-stimulation

The reason why some dogs develop displaced sexual behaviour may also be linked to an over-stimulation of the area in the brain that deals with sexual development in the early life of a puppy. This heightened stimulation may possibly occur during pregnancy, when the mother experiences a hormonal surge. A surge can also be triggered or learned if mature dogs around the developing puppy are prone to repeatedly displaying dominance through mounting behaviour or are performing mating behaviour within sight and physical contact of the puppy.

Addictive influence

There is an addictive element to displaced sexual behaviour in that naturally forming 'reward chemicals' or hormones such as dopamine (triggered by anticipation) and serotonin (reward) are produced at the same time. This hormonal stimulation (rewarding the pleasure centre in the dog's brain) then triggers the reflex act of mounting.

Human and canine influences

Understandably, a dog's displaced sexual behaviour often attracts the concentrated attention of the owner; people may admonish or laugh or shout at a dog when exposed to inappropriate mounting. In the early months of a puppy's life, this type of dramatic interaction, intervention and attention can promote or reinforce the promotion of sexual arousal. Exposure to human- or canine-based aggression or prolonged exposure to dominance-related aggression in the litter or with another dog at home have also been known to trigger displaced sexual behaviour.

Below: Dogs may use mounting behaviour to assert their dominance, which can also be achieved by standing above a rival.

Training

When your puppy is obedient, calm and controllable, he immediately becomes everyone's friend. Training a puppy is usually straightforward, although it can be more challenging when it involves large and boisterous breeds.

Creating associations

You can begin teaching a puppy to 'Come' from his earliest days. He will learn from your cheerful or enthusiastic tone of voice when addressing him by name that you are happy with him. His reward can be an enthusiastic stroke or pat and praise. If you repeatedly congratulate him, he will soon associate 'Come' with attention and praise. You can then introduce some simple training instructions. But bear in mind that it isn't the actual words that he will understand but the sounds and whatever actions or events that are immediately linked to them. When he hears 'Walkies' before a lead is attached to his collar, he will learn to associate the sound 'K' with the promise of a walk.

Problem puppies

Puppies that enjoy nothing more than a challenge may completely ignore any instructions and find something else to do. This is where motivation and a few tasty food treats can help. If when instructing your puppy to 'Come' he ignores you, try walking away – an action he won't be expecting. If training is proving difficult, introduce food rewards or clicker and reward-whistle training (see pages 74–75) to help promote obedience.

Reinforcement strategies

Your puppy will understand instructions such as 'Sit' more effectively when given in a low-toned voice. If you hold your hand up in front of you with a treat, he may naturally sit back in the hope of obtaining the food. This is the moment to say 'Sit' and to congratulate him and give a food treat. The timing of this interaction will encourage him to respond next time he hears the word 'Sit'. If your puppy avoids sitting when instructed, he may be challenging your control (see pages 64–65).

Above: *Always praise and stroke a dog for its obedience as this will act as a positive motivator and encourage him to respond to all training instructions.*

He will be constantly watching your facial movements in an attempt to understand what you require of him, so support your instructions with hand signals, such as:

'Come' – wave your hand towards you or pat your knee

'Sit' – hold your hand out with your palm facing down in front of him

'Down' – point down to the floor and draw him down from the sit position

'Move off' – point your hand forwards

'Walk to heel' and **'Stay'** – hold your hand by your side or with him held down.

During early lead training, introduce instructions such as 'Stop', 'Sit', 'Heel' and 'Wait', rewarding with food treats when he responds appropriately. While walking, if your puppy fails to remain close to your side and pulls, instruct him to 'Heel' in a firm, clear voice, drawing him nearer to your side. Once he has responded, give the 'Sit' instruction and only continue when he has obeyed. Your puppy will soon learn that pulling is unacceptable and that he has to accept your control.

Positive encouragement

Your puppy will always learn best if training sessions are enjoyable. If he senses that you are angry or disappointed with him, he will soon be discouraged from responding. It can take a number of attempts for a puppy to learn a new instruction. He may not always understand exactly what you require of him and any frustration or disappointment on your part will only confuse him further. Always reward him with a food treat, praise and a stroke when he responds correctly.

It is vital that you don't shout aggressively at your puppy or smack him, as these actions will be interpreted as conflict within the pack. In some instances, it may even encourage mistrust or aggression or nervousness. Always signal problem behaviour with a sharp, low-toned 'No' or with training discs (see page 75).

SHOULD I TAKE MY PUPPY TO CLASSES OR TRAIN HIM AT HOME?

Dog training classes can help socialize your puppy with others. Providing the sessions are fun and rewarding for you and your puppy, the benefits will be obvious. However, some of the most beneficial 'training' can be gained from throw and fetch games in your home or garden.

Below: *Most dogs will enjoy training sessions when food treats are offered as a reward for success.*

Above: This German Shepherd is wearing a receiver collar filled with citronella. A hand-held transmitter is used to trigger a behaviour-interrupting spray.

Training devices

There are various devices that can be successfully used in training sessions to interrupt or change your dog's problem behaviour in various ways, such as by positive reinforcement or negative association.

Remote-controlled scent collar

This is used as an aversion device in dealing with problem behaviour, to establish in a dog's mind an association between a negative event and an undesirable action. With the press of a button, the specially adapted collar unit will first send out a beep. If your dog does not respond, then the second and third button sends out a short or long, powerful blast of a citrus scent. This scent, because of your dog's super sense of smell, is usually strong enough to interrupt your dog's behaviour. Your dog will quickly associate the overwhelming scent with his behaviour and the effect can reduce and often stop it altogether. Most collars can be activated up to 300 m (328 yd) from your dog as it commences any behaviour that is considered antisocial or undesirable.

Clicker

This simple device consists of a thumb-sized plastic unit with a thin metal film, which, when pressed, sends out a double-click sound. Initially linked with food treats, this sound is used as a signal for reward, to reinforce good behaviour.

The science on which clicker training is based is known as 'classical conditioning', and relates back to Professor Pavlov and his famous 'association and effect' experiment carried out a century ago. With his laboratory dogs, he established an association between ringing a bell and offering food, which then became so powerful that on hearing the sound of the bell (an artificial signal), they salivated in anticipation of the food (a natural response) even when it wasn't being offered, the sound and the response becoming one. In the same way, the sound of the clicker becomes embedded in the dog's brain when it is associated with a special food treat, and in time, the double click *becomes* the treat, and so the signal can be used without food to reward good behaviour, both in the home or on walks.

It is advisable to introduce the clicker for the first time to dogs in a brief, simple, training-session in the home or garden. Call a dog by name, tell him to sit and sound the clicker immediately he begins to respond and sits. Follow the sound of the clicker by giving the dog a tasty 'food treat'. Initially, the reward linked to the sound of the clicker should be food-based (small pieces of tasty meat) but eventually the 'reward' does not need to be food but should be a pat or a verbal-congratulation 'Good boy', 'Good girl' or 'Good dog'. To retain its association with food it is possible to click before his daily food dish has been placed down.

Reward whistle

A dog-training whistle can be used to attract your dog's attention and help him respond appropriately to your instructions. Some owners prefer to use an audible whistle, while others work with the so-called silent whistle that has a pitch above our hearing range but within that of dogs. As with the clicker, begin by linking the sound of the whistle with a significant food reward combined with attention and fuss. The reward whistle should be used randomly around the home or garden during this initial exposure period, so that your dog doesn't associate it with any particular event, such as walks, visitors coming to your home or normal mealtimes. Stand in another room from the dog and sound the whistle. Once he responds positively with a recall and sit, reward his obedience with either a very special food treat and a pat or verbal praise or a brief toy-retrieval play session. All good behaviour can then be signalled with a click and treat. In this way, in your dog's mind, the reward whistle will become the promise of a click and treat if he responds promptly to the sound.

Training discs

This device, developed by the late John Fisher and now sold as Mikki Dog Training Discs, consists of five brass, tambourine-like discs, about 5 cm (2 in) in diameter, held together on a cord. When they are calmly shaken, they make a very distinctive sound. As with the clicker, the training discs are used as a sound signal but in this case one that is associated with the removal of a reward, that is, the exact opposite of the clicker. Once a dog has associated the sound of the training discs with the withdrawal of a food treat, they can easily be used to deal with many simple problem behaviours, such as jumping up, growling and biting.

Below: The clicker, once it is associated with food treats, can be used by all family members to signal appropriate and obedient behaviour.

In the home

Interactive behaviour

The social animal within your dog wants to interact with you. If you have plenty of time and energy, then all his attention needs can be served. He will probably interact differently towards young children and older family members because he realizes that they are less likely to fulfil his basic needs. His strongest desire for attention and interaction is usually reserved for those who feed and walk him regularly.

The need for attention

The sense of social pack structure that is genetically programmed into your dog's brain is probably the secret behind the millions of successful relationships between owners and their dogs around the world. Your dog needs to be a part of a social group and your family provides a similar structure to the canine pack in many ways. There is usually one or two people at the head of every family, in the same way that the *alpha* male and female lead the canine pack. Most households include people of different ages and sex that live, eat, sleep and have fun together, and a dog usually finds his place and thrives within this hustle and bustle of everyday human life.

He may follow you about the home and run to you when you return from a period of absence. Once you are seated, he will lie down at your feet or, if allowed, rest next to you on the sofa.

Toys for interaction

Once a dog has mouthed a toy, it is marked with his scent and therefore belongs to him. If your living room floor is littered with such toys, your dog is likely to have his particular favourite and might pick this one up first to offer in greeting. He may only show an interest in a toy if you try to pick it up before he has had a chance to take hold of it. In the milder forms of competitive behaviour between a dog and his owner, he will usually always want what you have, often initiating tug-of-war games to regain possession.

Your dog may wait until you are preoccupied with other aspects of home life and then suddenly turn up with the toy, which he will drop at your feet or on your lap. This is because he has learned previously as a puppy that you might interact with him in these situations. Some dogs display possessive behaviour over toys, by taking and hiding them away only to growl at encroaching family members, or they will use them to challenge owners (see pages 64–65) over leadership or levels of strength.

Left: *Dogs will deliberately take up positions that are close to their owners as they await interaction for play, feeding or walks.*

Right: *It is natural for many gundog breeds to carry toys as they would prey. Some use this behaviour to gain their owner's attention.*

QUESTIONS AND ANSWERS: ATTENTION SEEKING

How can I prevent my dog attention seeking all the time with all his toys?

This can be achieved by ignoring all your dog's various attention-seeking behaviours unless he picks up and carries a designated toy. Once he does this, he should receive your attention, but if the toy is dropped, ignore him. In time, your dog should learn that holding the toy is the way to solicit your response. Avoid using it as an interactive play item between you to prevent it from becoming associated with competition. The toy should be of a convenient size and always available for your dog to pick up and carry, while ensuring that he doesn't have the chance to gain access to other inappropriate attention-seeking items. Keep all other dog toys in a box.

Is my dog's attention seeking saying that he needs more from me?

Some dogs may develop antisocial or unhealthy behaviours having learned that performing them will usually attract their owner's attention. Once a reaction is gained from a family member, the dog's behaviour is then reinforced. Sometimes attention-seeking behaviour involves hyperactivity such as mouthing or scratching at an owner. In other instances, he may bite his paw or tail, or engage in repetitive or obsessive and compulsive behaviours including tail chasing, repetitive barking and excessive grooming (see pages 148–149).

Visitors and visiting

In our sociable world, we naturally welcome visitors and like visiting others, and in this way your dog is the same. Any new person coming into your home is a cause for excitement and he will respond according to his personality. Outgoing dogs will be enthusiastic, whereas a timid dog may initially hide. Visiting other homes is usually also viewed as a good opportunity to do some meeting and greeting.

Enthusiastic greetings

Your dog will enjoy any social activity that can involve him. He wants to be a part of the human–canine pack and needs interaction with you as owner. When visitors come to your home, he knows there will be competition for attention, so he will usually perform his best interactive skills to gain an advantage, such as vigorous tail and bottom wagging, lots of hand licking and maybe a few play barks. He may even show hyperactive behaviour in the form of jumping up.

Any regular visitors, and even those infrequent ones known to your dog over a long period, may be greeted with extra enthusiasm, as he probably views them as part of your extended pack. He may even carry his favourite toy to act as a greetings card for your visitors and then wait patiently until they are seated before presenting them with his gift. This behaviour equates to him locating a game bird in the wild. He views this task as part of his contribution to the pack, and he knows not to eat the 'game bird' but to carry it back and surrender it in a submissive act. This behaviour has been selectively bred for in many breeds by hunters since the early days of domestication.

Exploring new places

Visiting other homes offers your dog a chance to meet other people, their dogs or other pets and the rooms of another dwelling, and is probably seen as something of an adventure playground to a dog. Some dogs display excitability when taken into other homes and this is because they often arrive after a journey already in an aroused state with all their senses heightened. Your dog will be very keen to sniff out every corner and explore any garden area. Most dogs will leave their mark in another garden in the form of urine or faeces. This is territorial behaviour and if another dog or cat lives in the home you are visiting, he may enthusiastically over-mark in the same places they have already scented.

Above: An enthusiastic welcome is given and received, with the dogs competing for the visitor's attention with tails wagging.

Far right: When dogs explore a new territory they will often use urine to scent-mark, leaving a message for any other dog that might come along.

HOW CAN I CURB MY DOG'S ENTHUSIASM WITH VISITORS?

Changing hyperactive behaviour in dogs – jumping up at or displaying fearfulness towards family, visitors and strangers – can be achieved by setting up and repeating pre-planned, controlled scenarios. Ask a friend or neighbour, who should be confident with dogs, to play the role of visitor and plan the time at which they ring the doorbell and enter your home, which allows you the opportunity to work on your dog's behaviour.

1 The moment the doorbell rings, sound or make a signal for reward (a whistle that has already been used randomly and is linked to a food treat, see page 75, a pat or verbal praise).

2 Call your dog to you and 'condition' a controlled response, that is, once he has responded to the recall and your instruction to sit, reward him with a food treat.

3 If your dog's excitability is too great to control, prevent his immediate access to the visitor by the use of a dog gate to help slow down the initial interaction.

4 Ask the person to visit or approach on a number of occasions so that you can work on having your dog in the sit position in readiness. In this way, you are not pressured to deal with the visitor before the dog or have to remove him to another room while you deal with a real visitor.

5 Allow your visitor to offer him a food treat as a reward if he remains calm in a sit position. If giving your dog a food treat encourages hyperactive behaviour, use a clicker (already associated with food treats) to signal reward (see page 74).

Above: Most dogs thrive on retrieval games with their owners, but some will use play interaction to challenge them.

WHAT IF MY DOG ISN'T INTERESTED IN RETRIEVING TOYS FOR ME?

Some breeds respond better to retrieval games than others, but with patience and persistent encouragement and enthusiasm on your part, most dogs can be taught to chase after and retrieve a play item, such as a hard ball, bone, dumb-bell or frisbee. Once the toy has been thrown and successfully retrieved by your dog, he should be instructed to sit and be made to give up the object immediately. If he returns on your recall, give him a big cuddle and then instruct him to sit for his reward. The reward can be given in the form of a pat, verbal praise or a food treat, or initially a combination of all three. While you can encourage your dog to retrieve a toy by your enthusiasm alone, it is best to use a reward to prompt him to release the toy that he has brought back to you.

Toys

Dog toys have their parallels in remnants of the kill in nature. In the wild, the object of play might be a bone or piece of skin, and these are replaced in our homes by a wide range of items, some more durable than others. Ensuring that your dog gets the best out of his toys is quite simple: don't let him be in charge of them.

Carry toys

Most of the gundog breeds like to carry a toy. This behaviour is an obvious replacement for carrying a game bird, and many dogs learn to use toy carrying to gain their owner's attention. When your dog enthusiastically brings you a toy as he is greeting you, he is offering this interaction in the hope of pleasing you.

Staying in control

Toys can be an important part of a dog's day and it is possible to use them positively during interaction. However, some dogs will show possessiveness (growling) over a toy in order to challenge your leadership. A toy can also be used as an attempt to gain your attention at times when you are not able to offer him your interaction.

Dogs that want physically to challenge their owners will enjoy tug-of-war games best. The toys developed for pulling should only be introduced on an infrequent basis and should not be used if there are any issues of aggression or hyperactivity, as they can encourage your dog to test his strength against yours. Outdoor games that last no longer than five to ten minutes are best, and these can be developed using a ball or frisbee.

It is important that such games are brought to an end on your instruction, for example, by saying 'Game over', with the toy in your possession, and that it is then replaced in the toy box. In removing the toy, you are demonstrating your dominance or leadership, and by putting toys away and out of your dog's reach, you can prevent him becoming possessive over them.

Scent games

Most dogs enjoy scent games, although breeds that are highly scent orientated, such as the Bloodhound, Dachshund, Beagle and Basset, will respond most enthusiastically to them.

Begin by introducing different items but especially new toys to your dog, using a phonetic sound, such as 'B' for ball, 'F' for frisbee or 'T' for teddy, to identify each one. Initially mark the one chosen to be located and retrieved with a strong-smelling food treat. Throw the items together and announce which he should bring back. Reward him enthusiastically, either by saying 'Yes' brightly or sounding a clicker (see page 74), as he sniffs the one you have marked and praise him for bringing the correct one back. If he returns with an incorrect one, gently say 'No' and ask him to try again. This will encourage him to make a choice based on your instructions, therefore challenging him mentally rather than physically. In a similar vein, you can also scent one of a series of numbered cloths with underarm scent and then place them on the ground in a line. Keep him in the sit position until you give him the command to fetch or find the scented cloth, giving lots of praise and a reward when he returns with the correct one.

Below: Terriers enjoy nothing better than using their strong scent-tracking abilities. This dog is poised for a search-and-find game among the cushions.

Marking and barking

On walks or their home territory, dogs use their bodily wastes to leave their mark, which is a message to other dogs that this place belongs to him and his pack. When your dog barks in the home, he is drawing your attention to something that he perceives to be potentially dangerous.

Above: Alert-barking in dogs is territorial behaviour and its intended use in nature is to warn pack members (or you as pack leader) of potential threats.

Far right: Male dogs place a urine mark as high as possible perhaps to deceive another dog into thinking they are much larger than they are.

Territorial marking

Your dog might show a particular interest in a patch of grass when out on a walk where a female has urinated, because he can scent whether or not she is ready for mating. If he is very stimulated by the smell, he may crouch down to over-mark with his own urine. Some dogs will even roll over and rub in the scent to carry it away with them. Dominant male dogs will mark almost every vertical object they encounter.

Anal gland scenting

Wild dogs use their anal glands, either side of the anal opening, to add extra musk-like scent to faeces or to leave a strong scent mark on saplings or clumps of grass. Scientists have suggested that the anal gland is inoperative in domesticated dogs, although some appear to suffer from impacted and infected anal glands. There seems to be a correlation between dogs that show signs of being territorially insecure (see below) and anal gland activity. In many cases, they need to have the glands emptied by a veterinary surgeon, otherwise they smell strongly and drag their bottoms on the ground while performing a rowing-like action with their back legs, which can be mistaken as an indication of worm infestation.

Territorial barking

Selectively bred for in domestication, territorial barking and growling is usually displayed around the home and is directed at a perceived threat, often triggered by the doorbell. Aspects of territorial aggression can be seen in most breeds, but especially in rescue or adopted dogs and working breeds, particularly insecure individuals among many of the terrier or guarding breeds such as the German Shepherd Dog and livestock-controlling dogs including Collies.

Dogs displaying territorial insecurity have either experienced a change in ownership or have moved homes. Most re-homed or rescued dogs are hyper-alert and possess higher adrenaline levels than normal following the combined trauma of being rejected by an owner and being housed with other rescue dogs that are constantly barking. They then have to establish themselves in the new owner's territory and this change encourages territorial barking and over-dependency (see pages 114–115).

Repetitive barking

This is usually directed at delivery personnel and callers at the door but can also be aimed at people on foot, joggers, cyclists and cars passing by. These moving targets help to make the behaviour highly addictive because they leave the scene and appear to be dealt with and so a relieved dog receives a 'reward' fix. The subsequent imbalance in the levels of hormones, including adrenaline, dopamine and serotonin, appears to dominate neural activity, therefore the dog loses the ability to control decisions related to stimuli and perceived threats. This can eventually develop into an obsessive and compulsive disorder (see pages 148–149). Repetitive barking that occurs when an owner is away from home is linked to separation-related disorder (see pages 118–121).

HOW CAN I PREVENT MY DOG FROM EXCESSIVE BARKING?

Try to avoid the situations where an excited or aggressive response from your dog is likely to occur. This can be early mornings or evenings, but also after the postal delivery or when your dog encounters other dogs or strangers on walks. It might be when he has become excited or nervous at the arrival or departure of people, or when he considers that there is competition for his territory, toys or food or he is attention seeking.

Reduce his ability to patrol or guard windows, doors, gates or the garden (see page 117). If a dog is target barking in the garden, you may need to restrict his access temporarily. When he continues to bark, sound pre-associated training discs (non-reward), then quickly sound a clicker (reward) (see pages 74–75) the moment he stops, without giving him physical attention.

The right bite

There is an incredible range of foods available to the discerning dog owner today, including dried, semi-moist and canned foods. It is not your dog that buys the food, but if he could choose, which type would your dog prefer?

ADAPTABLE CARNIVORES

If you were to offer your dog the choice between rack of lamb and some apples, it is quite obvious which option he would choose. Dogs are primarily carnivores, which can be clearly seen in their wolf-like teeth, and yet they easily adapt to being omnivores.

Dogs in nature are known to eat almost any edible object in situations where shortages exist. Observations involving Italian feral dogs revealed that groups of them scavenged a great deal around human refuse areas and were observed feeding on long-dead livestock carcasses, including cattle and horses. Some were seen taking chickens or digging for small mammals. One group targeted foals and another pack of eight dogs were recorded as having taken large numbers of sheep. It is also known that dogs will eat berries from bushes, alongside some invertebrates including insects, spiders and beetles. Many owners report that their dogs will happily eat vegetables if offered them, and at least one Chihuahua has been known for his obsession with eating raw carrots!

DIET AND BEHAVIOUR

In a survey conducted by South African canine behaviourist Glynne Anderson (see page 160), 1,000 dogs were offered a change of diet, from prepared dog foods to raw meat, because of behavioural issues, including aggression. She determined that three-quarters of the sample number displayed improvements in behaviour following the change in diet and before any behavioural modification had been fully put into place. In Anderson's opinion, food is nature's natural drug and she even compares food with Valium or Prozac in its effectiveness in helping to calm a dog and encourage it to be more rested.

Just as research into diet and children with ADHD (attention deficit hyperactivity disorder) uncovered a linked between food additives in sugary drinks and food, and behaviour, it is suggested that dogs are similarly affected by what they eat. It is thought that some of the food colourings and additives found in most processed commercial dog foods might encourage hyperactive behaviour in dogs. Some experts believe that offering fresh or uncooked meat (or food that hasn't been processed for an extended shelf life) is far better than packaged food. Dogs can show less interest in dried, prepared foods, and this could be the reason why your dog may seem bored with his current diet if served this every day.

Above: Food represents an important energy resource and most dogs will not only eat a meat-based diet, but enjoy some fruits and vegetables, too.

WHAT SHOULD I FEED MY DOG?

Most dogs will eat anything placed in front of them to the point of clinical signs of hyperphagia (a compulsive eating condition); obesity in dogs is believed to be on the increase. Other dogs have a fussy attitude towards food, but it is difficult to assess if this is due to them disliking what is being offered to them or because a negative association has been formed with that particular food or food in general, perhaps related to excess competition for food in the litter or punishment linked to food by an owner.

The range of commercially prepared dog foods, from dried to moist, have a great advantage over a simple piece of meat because they contain all the necessary ingredients for canine health, including important vitamins and minerals. A variation in diet can be offered by the occasional addition of a few lightly cooked vegetables with a small amount of blanched minced meat stirred into the normal meal (see page 135). Uncooked meat takes longer to digest and a larger amount of enzymes and bacteria are needed in order to break down unprocessed food. Dogs are said to rest longer after eating raw meat.

Feeding

The most important resource to a dog is his food. In nature, there is no knowing where the next meal will come from, so when the opportunity arises, a feeding frenzy may ensue. Domestic dogs have adapted to a daily pattern of mealtimes, although even the best fed will drool at the anticipation of a new food source.

In anticipation

Whenever a dog smells food, he will usually salivate. This is a natural response because saliva is required not only to lubricate food and enhance its passage down the throat but also to carry important enzymes and bacteria that will help to facilitate its breakdown in the digestive system. Your dog cannot only smell food from a great distance, but he can also pick up visual and sound cues that tell him food is on its way.

Food boredom

Few dogs have to perform a task in order to be fed. This can be an issue with working breeds and food boredom can develop. In the home, the food dish is put down and, more often than not, remains there until it is refilled or cleaned away. Since your dog can simply forage as he suits, any potential for mental stimulus related to food is lost. Scientific research has shown that dogs in their natural state are known to spend up to 50 per cent of all active behaviour searching, locating, stalking, hunting, chasing and catching prey. In domestication, this group of important activities, directly linked to the most important resource of all, is usually reduced to walking up to and eating food from a dish.

HOW CAN I STOP MY DOG FROM GROWLING WHEN I GO NEAR HIS FOOD?

Dogs can display competitive or possessive aggression with regard to food. Research suggests that this behaviour can be triggered when a puppy has had to over-compete for food in a large litter or when he has not received the amount of nourishment he needs. Some dogs deliberately leave a small amount of food in the dish in order to return to it and display possessiveness over what remains. As soon as your dog has finished eating, remove the dish, even if he has not eaten all his food. If he doesn't eat within ten minutes of being offered food, remove the dish and try offering it again later. If you suspect that he will be excited or aggressive when you attempt to remove the food dish, distract him into another room before returning to remove it.

Above: *Saliva is produced as a natural response to a food stimulus and plays an important role in digestion for dogs.*

Food-foraging games

Instead of simply offering your dog his food in a dish or offering food scraps from your plate without requiring any effort on your dog's part, try organizing a foraging game.

1 Confine your dog in the home, behind a dog gate or a glass door, ideally in sight of the garden or area of the home where you will hide the food.

2 Place measured amounts of his normal daily food ration into paper cake cups, rice paper parcels or semi-sealed tubs and packets, but nothing too difficult to open.

3 Use the garden, or an appropriate area in the home, to hide at least half of his normal food ration, for example, under empty plastic plant pots. For the first game, make at least one of the portions fairly easy to locate, or, if in semi-sealed packets, easily accessible.

Above: Prevent food boredom by offering a healthy variation in diet and encourage foraging games where dogs can search out titbits.

4 Release the dog at the gate or doorway from where he can seek and locate the hidden food. Say 'Yes' brightly, sound a clicker (see page 74) and instruct the dog to search or 'find' the food. If your dog searches in all the wrong places, say very firmly 'No'. It is important to be ready to praise (or use a clicker and a whistle to signal reward, see page 75) when a dog has located the food. Over time, the divisions of food can be increased and made more difficult for him to find or gain access.

Above: Dogs rarely enjoy being parted from families but most understand that an owner will return for them.

Far right: Many dogs placed in boarding kennels will repeatedly bark when first separated from their owners.

At the kennels

We can only guess what is going through a dog's mind after he has been deposited at boarding kennels and his owner has left. The journey to the kennels probably represents a human–canine pack-hunting episode to the dog, and he may think that his owner has then gone off to 'hunt and forage' without him.

Responses to separation

Research suggests that dogs miss their owners from the moment of separation and that, if there are to be any problems in the period of owner absence, they will begin almost immediately. Some dogs simply lie down and wait patiently for their owner to return. Others begin barking repeatedly and almost endlessly in the vain hope that their owner will return and continue the relationship as normal. Other dogs scratch and chew at any available object in what represents a practical way of dealing with canine stress. A few toilet immediately in an emotional response to being left behind in a new territory that has yet to be marked.

Experience will teach a dog that has been kennelled on a number of occasions that his owner will eventually return. Once an owner comes back into view, the dog understands that normal life will resume. The first-time kennelled dog must be fairly confused at the situation he finds himself in. Depending on age and personality, most dogs will adapt to being housed temporarily in a strange place. The younger dog with a calm personality will adapt best. Older dogs don't enjoy any changes from the comfort of normal routine. They eat little and often pine for their owners from the moment of separation until they return. Most dogs have plenty of fat reserves to live off and a week or more of fasting or eating the bare minimum required probably has a beneficial effect on their health.

QUESTIONS AND ANSWERS: BOARDING DOGS

How can I make kennelling my dog a better experience?

Adopt a no fuss, no emotion and no eye contact strategy during the transfer to avoid communicating your anxieties directly to the dog. Try to organize all the necessary paperwork in advance so that a fast getaway can be made. It is a mistake to cuddle and tell your dog that you will be back soon; any emotional fuss and language used will only cause confusion. It is also a mistake to take your dog on a long walk prior to the separation because the contrast between your absence and presence will only be exaggerated. An old, freshly scented garment of yours (worn around the home or slept in overnight) can be left with the dog as a comfort blanket.

How can I tell if my dog has been unsettled by a stay in the kennels?

If your dog returns from the kennels and his usual personality has markedly changed even after a few days back home, this can be taken as a clear sign that a kennel-related trauma has occurred. If he refuses to eat or withdraws from normal social life in the home, such as hiding away under tables, chairs, beds or other furniture, then it is advisable to seek professional advice from your veterinary clinic or animal behaviourist before his behaviour becomes habitual and progresses.

My dog is obviously not happy in kennels. What are the options?

Research suggests that dogs prefer to remain in the place they know and feel secure in, so ask a family member, a friendly neighbour or friend to act as dog-sitter for the holiday period. However, it is important to advise them not to fuss the dog too much because this can promote attachment behaviour. Provide them with a timetable of feeding and general instructions. Some localities have a vetted local agency that can provide a home dog-sitter. Another alternative is for your dog to stay at a family member's or friend's home. They can also stay in a family home with the aid of a short-term, personal dog-sitting service.

Moving home

How your dog views moving home may be dictated by his personality. Moving from one home to another is classified as one of the five major stress-inducing factors in human life. Any anxieties you may feel will be transmitted to your dog. Calmness is therefore the key to a smooth and successful transition.

Responses to change

Dogs don't like change any more than most people, but a new territory can either be enthusiastically explored or viewed with trepidation, depending on their age and personality. It is obviously not possible to explain to a dog why, how and when a house move is taking place, but dogs can sense big days. They can hear household items being

HOW CAN I MAKE THE TRANSITION EASIER FOR MY DOG?

First, the calmer you are prior to and during the move, the better it is for your dog. If there are professional movers involved, it is best to create a temporary dog zone rather than putting your dog in boarding kennels. Set up the zone within a small room in the house with his basket or covered indoor kennel and a talk radio programme playing, to provide a 'den effect' in a calm and secure place. Instead of a closed door, install a dog gate so that he can stand and see what is going on if he wants, while being kept safely away from potential hazards, such as when the removal van is being loaded. Replicate this dog zone in the new house so that people are free to come and go through open doors without fear of the dog bolting.

Take your dog on several short walks spread across the day of the move rather than a single extended walk, as they require less energy and so the dog will be generally calmer. It is wise to feed sparingly in case the journey or the emotional upset causes a digestive problem. With dogs of a nervous disposition, transfer urine-soaked kitchen paper together with a small amount of faeces from the old home to the new home, out of sight of the dog. When he arrives at the new place, he can smell his own scent already there and be encouraged to over-mark and claim the new territory as his own.

Above: *Dogs will become anxious when they see empty rooms in familiar surroundings. To prevent stress, offer a quiet 'Dog only zone' with a bed in the old and new home while the practicalities of moving are carried out.*

packed away as well as the excitement and stress in voice tones. They can probably smell the pheromones linked to human euphoria and apprehension, and they must realize that a home full of boxes and empty rooms means some kind of change is coming. Young dogs easily adapt to change; it would happen in nature when a pack decides to move on in search of new feeding grounds or the chance to locate a safer den area. The home move is not much different for a dog in this respect.

Early investigations

Dogs usually investigate a new home alongside the owner. In unfamiliar territory, the pack leader will undoubtedly show the way, from room to room and then back again, until familiarity breeds increasing confidence. If a dog is bounding around, then the house move will be taken in his stride. If he appears skulking and suspicious in his general disposition, then the transfer may not be going so smoothly for him. Any initial explorations should be carefully supervised, especially if your dog is a natural escape artist and inclined to run off at the first opportunity.

Establishing his new territory

One of the earliest acts a dog performs in a new territory is marking as he explores the near outdoors. Dogs will often perform urine scenting over and over again when exposed to areas of garden, paths, fences and trees for the first time, and will continue sniffing and scenting for some hours. Once accessed and marked, the new home territory is claimed safe and can then be defended. His first attention bark may be one of several events that announce the beginning of the home becoming yours. Once it is time for smaller household items to be unpacked, your dog might show his natural curiosity. Alternatively, he may just lie down and wait patiently for the moment his toys or food dish appear.

Below: This dog is taking a keen interest in unpacking. A tea break would be the ideal time to introduce him to a food- or toy-foraging game in his new home.

The great outdoors

Meeting other dogs

The dog walk is a replacement activity for hunting and foraging. For most dogs, it is the most exciting event of their day. Not only does it involve a journey with you as pack leader, but it also involves lots of excitement, including locating the scent of other animals, meeting people and, perhaps best of all for the social dog, encounters with other dogs.

Encounter factors

Dogs usually enjoy interacting with other dogs. A chance to run with the pack is the canine equivalent to children playing together in an adventure park. But how your dog behaves with other dogs when they are encountered on walks depends on several factors. One primary consideration is your dog's personality type. If he is sociable or submissive, and has been content and secure around other dogs from his earliest days, the nature of the encounter is almost completely dependent on how the other dog and his owner behave. A secondary factor is whether one or both dogs are restrained on leads. This is because dogs that are insecure or dominant are more inclined to display hyperactivity or aggression towards other dogs when either is on the lead. This may be because they are frustrated by being held back from exploring and encountering or that one of the dogs interprets the restricted movement of another dog when restrained on the lead as being aloof, threatening or even dominant.

Open encounters, good and bad

If your dog has the opportunity to run freely in open spaces with another dog, a series of body postures will first be displayed (see pages 28–29). If the social interaction is mutually positive, there will be plenty of tail and bottom wagging, sniffing and standing while being sniffed, occasionally some licking (often with both dogs alternating in a heads-to-bottoms position) and submission (turning over on to the back) or play bowing as an invitation to run and play. If the encounter is to be an awkward one, there will be a no-sniffing signal of dominance – standing still away from the other dog with the body line stiffened, with no invitation to sniff – possibly along with a warning growl, with neck ruff and hackles raised, tail stiffened and ears erect in a doggy stand-off. In this case, it might be best to leave the scene with your dog.

Making friends

Your dog may meet the same dogs over and over again, especially if walks are taken at a set time and in the same area. Your dog will come to know the other dogs and will want to run with them at every opportunity. Dogs love to race each other like children do in the playground. It is advisable to use a whistle to signal the end of a play session (when he returns, give him a fuss and a food treat), so that when it is time to resume your walk, it is not controlled by when your dog wishes to stop playing and return to you.

WHY DO SOME DOGS SHOW AGGRESSION TOWARDS MY ONCE-FRIENDLY DOG?

Now he is starting to show aggression towards dogs he was previously happy to play with. This behaviour means that either your dog has experienced dog aggression (known as intraspecific aggression) or has developed a fearfulness of other dogs. If your dog has been attacked by another, this experience is likely to make him wary, just as a person who has been mugged on the street will be anxious about it happening again every time they step outside. It can also often promote a 'get in first' behaviour that is often referred to by behaviourists as 'fear-based aggression'. Some fighting breeds, such as the Staffordshire Bull Terrier or the Shar Pei, may have higher levels of natural aggression and are therefore more likely to react aggressively if the dog version of social etiquette, when to sniff and when not to sniff, has not be adhered to.

Left: *When out on a walk, scenting and sniffing is the canine way of greeting and meeting for dogs.*

Below: *These dogs may be signalling an acceptance for mutual sniffing but tails, if held high, can also signal a warning.*

Solutions for outdoor problem behaviour

There can be situations in a dog's life when it is difficult for owners to separate problem behaviours that require basic training from psychological conditions that need both understanding and clinical treatment.

PROBLEM BEHAVIOUR	TRAINING SOLUTION
Chases after other dogs to play	Work on brief sessions with the clicker and reward whistle (see pages 74–75) using a special retrieval item or favourite toy in and around the home. Use tasty food rewards and lots of fuss and attention after each retrieval or exchange from dog to owner to help reinforce a positive association with the interaction. Once established, take the item and clicker or reward whistle on walks and use to help motivate recall.
Attacks other dogs	Use a remote-controlled scent collar as an aversion device (see page 74) in a scenario where controls can be put in place.
Selective recall	Work on clicker and reward-whistle training in and around the home as above to motivate recall on walks.
Running away and not recalling	Use a remote-controlled scent collar as an aversion device (see page 74) in a scenario where controls can be put in place.
Pulling on the lead	Use a padded head-control collar (see page 137), rather than a chest harness, which can encourage the dog to pull from his chest (often his strongest area) to test his strength against his owner. Introduce clicker training (see page 74) to reward not pulling.
Jumping up or lungeing at strangers or other dogs	Work with the clicker and training discs in sessions in and around the home (see pages 74–75). Then use training discs to interrupt jumping up or lungeing at in a controlled scenario where a friend plays the role of the approaching person, with a dog if that is part of the problem. Sound the clicker when his behaviour has been successfully countered.
Chasing wild animals, livestock, vehicles, cyclists, joggers, etc.	Work on clicker and reward-whistle training in and around the home as above to motivate recall on walks. A remote-controlled scent collar (see page 74) can interrupt the behaviour and recall can be improved by reward-whistle training (see page 75). In the case of dealing with addictive chasing of livestock, vehicles, cyclists, joggers etc., where the dog and people are put in danger, it is important to seek professional advice.
Panic behaviour/fear-based running way	Use a long, lunge-type rope (see page 141) attached to the collar on walks, which can be used to reel the dog in or bring him to a halt when he starts to bolt. Otherwise, seek professional advice.
Eating sticks or branches	Take a new retrieval toy on walks and use it together with a reward whistle (see page 75) to capture his attention. Once gained, offer him the chance to carry or play with the toy briefly. Permitting the chewing of sticks increases the risk of mouth injuries and allows your dog to dominate an item that is not under your control.
Scavenging carcasses	Use a remote-controlled scent collar as an aversion device (see page 74).

Left: Who is taking who for a walk? Some dogs pull on the lead and simply need training whereas some problem behaviours require treatment.

Meeting strangers and young children

During walks with your dog, there will be times when you encounter people, maybe a lone stranger or a family enjoying a stroll. If your dog is on the lead, the control of his subsequent behaviour is entirely in your hands, but if he is off lead, the success of the encounter will depend on his personality and how strangers react when he approaches.

HOW DO I ENSURE THAT MY DOG BEHAVES WELL TOWARDS STRANGERS AND CHILDREN ON WALKS?

Make sure that your dog is not encouraged to jump up at adults or children by keeping this behaviour in check with your own family members and friends. Praise and reward sitting and calmness to promote good manners. Teach your dog to come back when instructed in random sessions on walks and offer a special food treat and a fuss when he responds. This will allow you to bring the recall instruction into play whenever people are approaching.

If your dog has a habit of displaying hyperactivity or jumping up at strangers or children, ask a friend to play the role of an approaching stranger and to use training discs (see page 75) if he starts to behave boisterously. Children in your own family can play the role too. If your dog responds positively, offer him a food treat and a congratulatory stroke for being well behaved.

Above: Dogs can be encouraged to show calmness when encountering other dogs on walks through special training.

Right: Unpredictable behaviour around children should be controlled but most dogs view known children as puppies and will usually display gentle behaviour.

The personality factor

Meeting people on walks is all part of the fun for sociable dogs, and most view strangers as amiable animals. Again, as with meeting other dogs, one of the major influences on how your dog behaves towards people is his personality. Some dogs, absorbed in the wonders of 'hunting and foraging' with the human–canine pack, will blissfully ignore other people on walks and only relate to their owners and family. Others, especially gregarious dogs that thrive on interaction and live within a family-orientated group, will usually approach a stranger or another family enthusiastically.

Strangers' attitudes

Another important factor is how the people he encounters view him. The interaction may even be encouraged if the strangers are accompanied by a dog and both owners and dogs are sociable. On another day, if an encounter with strangers proves fruitless from your dog's point of view in that they ignore him, he will normally continue on your route. If the strangers are dog-friendly and encourage him, he is more likely to pause and accept some form of contact. If the strangers appear to be dog phobic, instantly recall your dog to prevent any potential upset or confrontation.

Breed influence

How others view your dog is almost entirely dependent on whether they are dog-friendly or not. However, some breeds are more likely to encourage interaction from strangers than others, and, especially if your dog is still a puppy – most children cannot resist the opportunity to stroke a puppy. The chances of encouragement from other people are probably greater if your dog is a small to medium-sized breed. Walking with a huge dog, such as a Rottweiler, is more likely to encourage caution on the part of strangers and children than if you are accompanied by an ambling Golden Retriever.

Selective hearing

For a fun-loving, happy dog, the world is his adventure playground. In the great outdoors, there exist the most special smells and wonderful animal scents. If he is lucky, there may be another dog to play with. But better still, the walk may offer the opportunity to chase wildlife. Once the scent from an animal is picked up by your dog, his sense of obedience may vanish as fast as a mouse.

Above: *A dog's natural sense of inquisitiveness can lead him into all kinds of excitement or trouble, including jumping up on to the table.*

Far right: *Once an interesting scent has been located some dogs simply follow their nose and ignore any owner instructions, especially recall.*

Encouraging interaction and recall

During walks, unless you are deep in thought or conversation, you and your dog will probably be half-focusing on each other; this is the fun of mutual exploration, even if the walk is along the same well-trodden path. Some owners routinely carry a retrieval toy or a tennis ball to help make the walk more interactive and to encourage recall training. Others allow a dog to collect sticks from the ground that the dog enjoys being thrown for him to retrieve. However, branches can cause damage to teeth and gums if the wood splinters, so it is much safer to use a toy instead.

Overwhelming distractions

If your dog spies or smells a wild creature, the recall can prove very difficult, as it is much less exciting for him to return than to follow the animal's scent tracks. The moment of running off can happen before you have had the chance to call his name. All the usual rules of walks can be forgotten as your dog races off on the chase.

Personality factors

Confident dogs, especially those that know the direction you are walking in, will often run on ahead, and it is at these moments that an interesting distraction can trigger a dog to disappear from view. If you call him, your dog may show selective hearing or the 'I will come back when it suits me' attitude. Some dogs can be within visual distance and still ignore a name call, looking back at their owner and then sniffing the grass a little longer. In these situations, the dog is challenging his owner like a naughty child. Many dogs run forwards only to return immediately, often at every stage of the walk, to 'tune in' and check on which direction the pack leader may want to go in. Dogs lacking in confidence outdoors will usually keep close by an owner as they look for reassurance and direction.

QUESTIONS AND ANSWERS: TURNING A DEAF EAR

My dog often ignores me when I first call him. How can I tackle this disobedience?

It is important to train your dog to respond to a whistle around the home from his earliest days (see page 75). When the dog responds, it is vital to reward him with praise or a cuddle and perhaps an exciting food treat to motivate him to come back on those occasions when you really need him to return. Take him on a walk where he hasn't been before and work with the reward whistle; you are more likely to have success when he isn't sure about the ground and intended direction.

What should I do when my dog has been frightened on a walk and runs away?

Dogs with a nervous disposition can be sound sensitive. But any dog may hear an unusual noise that unexpectedly triggers his flight response. The feared noises can be gunshots, thunder and even hot-air balloon burners. This adrenaline-driven behaviour, known as the 'flight or fight response' (see pages 24–25), quite literally takes over the dog's brain and forces him to switch into survival mode. Some dogs, when confronted by a fearful event, will run until either they find their way home or to the car or stop through exhaustion. This behaviour is almost impossible to interrupt. If your dog is prone to the flight response, a reward whistle (see above) used together with a remote-controlled scent collar (see page 74) can be successful if the trigger for flight is anticipated and the strategy is used early enough.

Responding to traffic

Dogs mostly dismiss road traffic as non-organic moving metal lumps of little interest. However, your dog's eyesight has evolved to detect movement rather than detail, and he may find a noisy car a distraction that irritates him or something suspicious that needs to be controlled or even chased off.

Early exposure

You would normally begin a dog's exposure to road traffic from his earliest days and this is particularly true if you live in an urban environment. In some cases, the first exposure to traffic for your dog would have been when you returned home with him in the car from the breeder who had sold you the puppy. For many dogs and owners, this day presents an exciting experience. Owners will be full of a mixture of optimism, anticipation and concern. Cars and trucks are travelling by as you make this special journey, but your puppy may be sleepy and uninterested or, in contrast, he may be confident enough to watch the world passing by from the car window.

Usually, a dog's first real exposure to traffic will be during early lead walking, when he is being taught to sit at kerbs or at road or street junctions. Over a period of time, most dogs become desensitized to the sound and movement of passing vehicles. Your dog's view is that if they don't bother you, they probably won't bother him either. The walk through the park or fields where he can run and play will be joyfully anticipated and the car journey in between just the tiresome or exciting prelude.

Car chasing

Some dogs become obsessed with the movement of traffic. This behaviour is stimulated by speed and turning wheels, which encourage a programmed motor response in the brain. This is based on a natural reaction to detecting movement,

MY DOG SEEMS TO BE SCARED OF TRAFFIC AND PULLS AWAY FROM THE DIRECTION IN WHICH WE WOULD NORMALLY COME TO A MAIN ROAD. WHAT CAN I DO?

Rescue dogs with a mixed experience of traffic or those dogs that have been inadvertently exposed to unpleasant or frightening events relating to traffic can make a negative association with busy roads and vehicles. For example, as a disorientated stray, a dog could have been faced with struggling to survive crossing busy roads, or as a young dog, he may have been exposed to a car backfiring or the sudden release of a truck's air brakes. Once the association has been made, it can be difficult to erase with some insecure dogs.

You can use clicker-reward method of training (see page 74) to change your dog's experience of traffic from one that has a negative association to a more positive one. Initially, use the clicker calmly around the home, then gradually expose the dog to light traffic – quiet times in a local supermarket car park are ideal – in purposefully devised training walks and reward any calm responses with the clicker. Eventually, your dog can be exposed to increasing levels of traffic and again rewarded with the clicker for calmness.

usually of prey or fellow predators, which triggers an instant response. Many of the breeds that become obsessed or addicted to attempting to control or chase after the movement of road traffic (or even cyclists and motorbikes) already have a natural controlling instinct, such as livestock-controlling dogs like Collies and German or Belgian Shepherd Dogs, but it is also seen in many of the terrier breeds, where the behaviour is linked to a kill response associated with rodents. Once reinforced or promoted by the addiction, the behaviour can become extremely antisocial and a real danger to the targeted traffic and people.

Interrupting the chasing instinct can be successfully achieved by using a remote-controlled scent collar (see page 74) as an aversion device when the dog begins the response, then sounding a clicker as a reward (see page 74) when the dog stops. It is advisable, however, that owners seek specialist advice from an animal behaviourist (rather than a dog trainer) about tackling this problem.

Left: *Teaching a young dog to sit at kerb sides is about him learning the safe way to walk near and cross busy roads.*

Below: *Some dogs are 'attracted' to or fearful of the movement of passing vehicles. It is important to maintain a dog's attention in these situations.*

Scavenging on walks

Scavenging is one of the most natural behaviours for dogs to perform. They are opportunists and regard anything edible that can be gained by exerting little or no energy as a valuable food resource. Whether the scavenged item is a long-dead animal carcass or a week-old piece of pizza is irrelevant to them. The problem for you can be making your possessive dog give up his prized find.

Rural and urban finds

Life couldn't be better for your dog when he is off lead in an area of fields and forest. This environment becomes his domain, and while he might not know whether you are enjoying the fresh air, your dog happily accepts that this is a mutually beneficial activity. However, a chance discovery can turn some dogs into stubborn little monsters. This could be the remains of an animal freshly killed by a wild predator or more often an ageing carcass by the time your dog encounters it. Towns and cities can offer equally attractive fare for him to sniff out, such as the bones left over from a takeaway chicken meal lurking in a bag behind refuse waiting for collection, if he is fortunate, or just a discarded food wrapper if less lucky. He will cheerily crunch or lick all this up as though it were the best thing since you accidentally dropped your food on the floor and your dog claimed it.

Above: It is only natural for dogs to search out and locate potential prey animals during walks.

Right: Foraging in amongst the refuse can be exciting for a dog but can lead to health and behavioural issues when rotting or unsuitable food items are located and guarded.

Far right: When on a country walk, be ready for your dog to locate items he has scented in the undergrowth and introduce distraction methods, such as a favourite toy, to discourage him from eating them.

Responses to remains

Dogs deal with discovered remains in several ways. Some will take hold of a carcass and bring it – putrid and smelling – directly to their owner and present it, dropping it at their feet in the same way that a gundog would return with a game bird. Others will guard a fabulous find and will only end their vigil when an owner arrives at the spot, takes hold of their collar and drags them away. Then there are those dogs that grab the carcass and hold on to it as though they have not been fed in months. As owners approach, these dogs will often run away and then almost return – over and over again in some instances – as if to taunt those owners who are already frustrated by this behaviour. This is because, as rancid as the remains may be, they are the closest some dogs get to a real kill. Challenging behaviour can be shown towards an owner because, in the dog's mind, the winner gets to keep a rotting carcass.

Dogs can, in some instances, eat items that would quickly give humans food poisoning because they can call on special enzymes and bacteria to break down whatever is left to consume. However, even dogs can make themselves less than well through scavenging, so it is advisable not to allow them to eat rotting food.

Dealing with scavenging

If your dog becomes adept at seeking out nasty, rotting food on walks, it is wise to have something with you that might offer him an exciting alternative, and one in your control. This can be a favourite toy or a new one, but it can also be a ball or frisbee or a meat chew. Use a reward whistle around the home and link it to him gaining access to the item you have chosen (see page 75). After the association has been made around the home, the sound of the whistle and sight of the item can encourage a dog to give up his gruesome find. If a dog is displaying possessive behaviour over a carcass, it may be necessary to use a remote-controlled scent collar to interrupt the behaviour (see page 74) and then, once changed, a training whistle will usually bring about recall.

In the car

Most dogs happily take to travelling in vehicles from their earliest journeys. Road trips, either short or long, are usually made to somewhere of great interest and your dog wants to be a part of whatever you and his human–canine pack are organizing.

A dog's eye view

A great many dogs fall into a restful state when they travel in vehicles, which must be due to the comforting purr of the engine vibration. Some extroverts are at their happiest when they are hanging a tongue out of the window and taking in the cooling breeze. These dogs want to sit up infront by the driver and be in charge along with the pack leader, although this is inadvisable for their physical safety. Since a road journey often means a visit to the seaside or countryside, dogs view it as the ultimate 'hunting and foraging' with the pack experience.

A significant vehicle journey, if a part of a holiday, may even be the longest journey you and your dog will ever make together. If the trip is a short one to the local supermarket, 'the kill' will be transferred from a trolley to your car in the form of shopping bags. While it is clearly not your dog that kills or brings home the food, you have effectively hunted it down together.

Hyperactivity

Some dogs are hyperactive in cars. It could be that they sense that something exciting will happen at the end of the journey and they are simply enthusiastic about the whole process. Sometimes problem behaviour in cars is associated with an adverse reaction to the motion in puppyhood. In other instances, it is simply due to a lack of experience in travelling in the car, and excitement of the new gives way to hyperactivity.

It is important that your dog feels secure when in transit, so provide him with a partially covered travel crate or an equivalent canvas unit to fit in the rear passenger section or in the back of a hatchback, which also offers additional physical safety. In the case of a vehicle accident, where an open door could suddenly expose a possibly traumatized dog to heavy traffic, a travel crate will prevent a disorientated dog running off in flight response (see pages 24–25) or, more important, from being injured.

Above: A car journey often represents an exciting episode for a dog because it offers the chance to explore new places and territories.

Far right: Ideally, dogs are best journeying in travel crates or transit dog-bag style canvas units. This method of vehicle travel is far safer than a fixed harness.

MY DOG IS CLEARLY UNHAPPY WHEN TRAVELLING IN THE CAR, AND HE BARKS AND PANTS A GREAT DEAL. HOW CAN I IMPROVE THE SITUATION?

Change his negative association with car travel by the use of reward signals:

1 Develop a scenario that will take you and your dog through the basic steps of a short car journey. Enter the car, switch the ignition on but only move off if and when your dog is reasonably calm.

2 Stop the car after a few minutes. You, or a fellow passenger, should then confidently walk around the car. If your dog has remained calm, get back in and continue on the journey. Sound a clicker (see page 74) and praise any appropriate behaviour. If he shows signs of distress or hyperactivity, stop the car and take the dog out of the vehicle. Use the clicker repeatedly to reward the performing of an intensive number of instructions – 'Stop', 'Sit', 'Heel' and 'Walk on' – during a five-minute walk. Go back to the vehicle with the minimum of fuss and return home.

3 Make random short car journeys that are not associated with familiar walks or repetitive trips such as to the supermarket or relatives.

4 Once the first three steps have been accomplished, make a journey to a favourite walk area.

At each positive step, use the clicker to signal reward to your dog for appropriate behaviour. If he becomes distressed or over-excited at any point, end the session, but always attempt to find a positive behaviour to reward during or at the end of the session, either when you open the back of the vehicle or when your dog is instructed to sit upon leaving the vehicle. If he begins to display acute hyperactivity during the short journey, try correcting the behaviour with the use of training discs to signal non-reward (see page 75).

At the vets

Dogs view a veterinary clinic with a mixture of excitement and apprehension. As you approach the door, your dog will be assailed with the scents of strange dogs and other animals and the people who accompany them. There might be the sound of dog barking or a cat meowing. All this raises both the pleasure and alert levels of most dogs.

Scents and sensibility

If this is his first time in a veterinary clinic, there will be unfamiliar scents and the combined whiff of medication and sterile cleaning fluids for your dog's heightened sense of smell to experience. The nature of his association with this aroma and his own sense of welfare will depend on his past experience and, secondarily, his own personality. A calm dog will take even the most daunting episodes in his stride, while a nervous dog will be showing fear before his owner has led

HOW CAN I MAKE VISITS TO THE VETERINARY CLINIC LESS STRESSFUL FOR MY DOG?

If a dog has developed a negative association with visiting the clinic because of prolonged illness or from the effects of intrusive surgery, it can be possible to create a better association, but changing his perception needs small, careful steps.

1 Walk your dog past the clinic and then return and pass the doorway again. Pre-arrange for a nurse to come outside and be introduced to your dog. A special food reward should be offered or 'click and treat' (see page 74). If your dog isn't calm, break off and repeat the process over several visits.

2 Introduce your dog into a quiet waiting area before or after a clinic session. Ask various people from the clinic to approach your dog, praise him and offer 'clicks and treats' as rewards for sitting or relaxed behaviour. Don't let him be stroked at this stage. Ask people who don't work at the clinic to repeat the process so that your dog experiences a mix of people along with the staff. Exposure should last no longer than five to ten minutes, then leave with your dog. Repeat every day.

3 Enter the clinic and reward any relaxed behaviour. Then allow him simply to investigate other rooms – especially the examination room. Repeat several times in a week. Ask if the veterinary surgeon is available at some stage in his schedule to come outside the clinic, and make your dog sit and take a food treat.

4 Enter the clinic and allow a veterinary surgeon to examine your dog casually and briefly. Click and reward any relaxed behaviour with a food treat. Leave without any treatment. Repeat several times a week.

5 Once every stage has been successfully achieved, your dog can be taken into the examination room and treated.

It may also be possible to use the confidence of another dog to promote a change in your dog's behaviour. If another dog shows a disinterest in the feared event, your dog may consider the clinic visit less of a threat.

him through the doorway. Many veterinary surgeons will automatically muzzle a nervous dog to prevent the chance of fear-based aggression. If a dog has a history of displaying problem behaviour in the clinic, this information will normally be stored in its records.

Positive steps

It is understandable that if every time your dog visits the clinic, a nurse or veterinary surgeon uses a hypodermic needle or inserts a thermometer into his anus, he may not view the place positively. It is therefore a good idea to arrange the odd purely social visit prior to and in between routine examinations and vaccinations or boosters (see Steps 2–3 opposite). If your dog has undergone surgery, waking up following anaesthesia with an injury may leave a negative association. Your concern and his eventual recovery should eventually mean that the experience is not unduly traumatic.

Your own mood before the visit can act as a cue for your dog. If you are apprehensive, he will most likely sense this through your scent and skin pheromones, and may well conclude that there is something for him to worry about too. The calmer you are, the calmer your dog will be.

Above: *Dogs can become less wary about being handled by veterinary staff through owner calmness and positive experience.*

Far left: *A calm, relaxed dog will wait obediently while being treated, having little concept of what is happening during veterinary examinations.*

Antisocial behaviour

Over-dependency

It is delightful to own a dog that wants to be with you all the time. Your dog unconditionally loves you and his need to follow on your heels around the home confirms this. A close relationship between owner and dog is one way to view this behaviour, but over-dependency is another. When his shadowing results in occasions when you almost trip over your dog, it is time to review the extent of his attachment.

How and why it occurs

Over-dependency in dogs develops when an unhealthy attachment is formed with a person and the relationship results in separation problems. This 'hyper-attachment' can result in a dog displaying destructive behaviour and indoor toileting, as well as repetitive barking when an owner is absent. When a young dog has the security of someone with them in the home most of the time and this situation suddenly changes due to the owner's work or study commitments, the dog may not like these changes. The 'home-alone' issue can have a bearing on his behaviour when family are around as well as when they aren't (see pages 118–119).

Following your lead

Your dog needs to have a pack leader and he is happiest when you are strong and can calmly make the correct decisions, as easy or difficult as they may be. The decisions could simply amount to which route the walk is going to take, when food is available or when to sit before crossing a road. More complex decisions might be whether the approaching stranger is a threat or not, if it is safe to be off lead or when it is time to sleep. That type of

HOW CAN I STOP MY DOG FROM DEMANDING ATTENTION ALL THE TIME?

When your dog first begins to pester you, the natural reaction will be to push him away and say 'No' or tell him to 'Settle down'. This response could be viewed as rejection or a game to most dogs. Use a book or clipboard, kept handily down the side of the sofa, and introduce it as your dog approaches. Hold the book up to block off contact and turn it from side to side as he attempts to circumnavigate your obstacle. Eventually, your dog will walk away (perhaps to search for another member of the family who could be the weakest link) and eventually lie down. If clicker training is being used (see page 74), the moment he settles down, sound the reward signal. Your dog will then respect your control.

Above: Your dog should be a close and loyal companion, happy to relax with you but not overly dependent on your company.

Right: Close contact, such as sleeping in the same bed or alongside you on the sofa, can lead to insecurity when denied these, or similar, opportunities.

leadership from an owner is a replacement for the *alpha* male and female leaders that would guide the pack to hunting grounds or the best den site. However, follow-my-leader behaviour in dogs can get out of hand if the early signs of over-attachment are not recognized.

Independence and insecurity

Secure and contented dogs rarely need continual visual or sound contact with their owners. They will nevertheless respond to the sight of a dog lead or the rustling of a food bag in the kitchen by coming to an owner's side. But apart from these obvious cues that suggest there is an activity to attend

to, these dogs are happy to rest or wait for action in a favourite place.

In contrast, the dog that is constantly at the feet of his owner when he is walking through the home or sitting comfortably watching television is not just bonding and is quickly unsettled when close contact is interrupted. These dogs are often masters of attention seeking, repeatedly pawing, licking and nudging owners, and even bringing a toy to drop in their lap if the other actions don't have the necessary effect. If the owner gives in, attention seeking can become a problem, especially when visitors are bombarded by a hyperactive dog.

Fearfulness and hyper-alertness

We are all affected in one way or another by fear and our dogs are no different. It is irrelevant whether the object of the fear is real or an illusion because both can trigger our own 'fight or flight response' and the surge of adrenaline. Nervous behaviour can easily be viewed as simply part of a dog's personality and levels of alertness allowed to develop to a point where he is in a perpetual state of readiness.

How fear affects dogs

When a dog is fearful and his neck ruff and hackles stand up, back and tail stiffen and he barks or growls, he is displaying his reaction to being threatened. But when he responds in this way to an ironing board being put up or a toaster popping toast, it means that he is hyper-alert and frightened of more or less anything that is not under his control. A dog that is continually displaying fear-based aggression or withdrawn behaviour is in need of understanding and treatment.

It is not the noise alone that triggers such irrational responses in dogs. Many gundogs, such as Cocker and Springer Spaniels or Labradors and other retrievers, that would normally display an indifferent or casual reaction to gunfire in their working role, can just as easily show adverse reactions to everyday sounds and situations when they are suffering from a hyper-alert condition.

Causes of fearfulness

A dog that is reacting fearfully to normal daily household situations and domestic items will usually have been affected by any of a number of adverse influences. These include welfare problems at the litter stage such as illness, poor husbandry, inadequate diet, lack of social interaction or excessive competition in large litters. Other factors can be early removal from the mother, illness of the owner, house

Above: Dogs have a natural desire to guard and protect their home territory but some may develop territorial barking.

Right: The security provided by an indoor kennel or travel unit is related to den burrowing behaviour in nature.

HOW CAN I PREVENT MY DOG'S TERRITORIAL BARKING?

One of the most effective methods is to restrict his daytime access to vantage points such as front room windows, stair elevations or window ledges. It may also be necessary to install dog gates to keep him away from the hallway or in back rooms where he cannot patrol or guard. These are preferable to closed doors because they represent social exclusion, which leads to frustration. Also restrict him from having access to side or front gates where he can target passing people.

moves and the result of commercial puppy-farm breeding where care has been minimal. Adopted or rescue dogs can also possess abnormal levels of adrenaline and will often show more fear-based behaviour than those dogs that have enjoyed a happier life. The process of re-homing, involving changes in owner and home territory, will upset most dogs' routines, the obvious effect being the raising of alert levels.

Research has revealed that dogs with physical conditions that require intrusive surgery or prolonged veterinary treatment will also often have increased alert states. Dogs that have formed an extremely powerful bond with an owner and go on to develop attachment problems (see pages 118–119) often have an unusually heightened sense of fear.

Setting up a 'den' for a nervous dog (see page 120) will provide him with a comforting, secure retreat when unusual noise triggers the 'fight or flight response' (see pages 24–25). The 'den' should be established in a quiet area in the home that would become the dog zone.

Signs of fearfulness and hyper-alertness

The earliest sign of a dog suffering from abnormal levels of fear and being in a stress-related, hyper-alert state is often territorial barking – barking and chasing off any perceived threat, such as passing dogs, refuse collectors, postmen or motorcycles. This behaviour is rewarded in a unique way in that the intensity of relief gained by some dogs after their apparent success in seeing-off perceived threats is far greater than any benefit that may have been gained from their aggressive action. This can develop into highly addictive behaviour associated with an increase in hormonal activity if the frequency of aggression increases (see page 123). People and dogs often leave the scene following the bout of aggressive behaviour and this helps to reinforce the dog's perception that he has succeeded in chasing off the potential threat to their human–canine pack and territory.

Separation-related disorder

This condition in dogs is similar to separation anxiety in humans, which mostly occurs in over-dependent children who show symptoms of distress and anxiousness upon separation from a parent or guardian. Dogs can only display signs of the condition rather than symptoms because they cannot tell us how they are feeling.

How and why it occurs

Separation-related disorder is a stress condition and can develop when a dog has formed a powerful attachment to or over-dependency on an owner. There are several triggers for its onset including adoption, trauma caused by intrusive surgery, illness or accident, changes in an owner's work patterns, an owner's sudden absence or the loss of a pack member (human or canine), infirmity, nervousness and house moves.

The condition is seen most widely in rescue and re-homed dogs, where, since no one can explain to them why an attachment has been broken, they become afraid of losing another owner. Frequently, most of the problem behaviour occurs in the owner's absence or, in certain cases, when a dog is only visually separated from an owner, such as during night-time sleeping or when shut behind a door. In rare cases, the same behaviour can be shown when family members are in the home, which may, given their presence, disguise the true nature of the problem.

Above: Stress-grooming is often exhibited by dogs that are experiencing owner-attachment issues.

Right: Some dogs find the moment of owner separation hard to bear, watching as you leave from the door or gate, accompanied by a howl or whine.

Far right: When dogs howl during separation they are echoing the behaviour of their ancestors, the wolves.

Vocalization during separation

In the wild, repeated barking is used by dogs as an alert, but it can also be adapted to call to pack members, where whining constitutes a submissive plea. Whatever vocalization has been used by your dog when you are absent, when you return, however long that takes, he then considers his behaviour to have been successful. Some neighbours report dogs barking continually all day while their owners are away. One sign that this is happening in your absence is when you notice that your dog is drinking excessive amounts of water. Stress and repetitive barking leaves a dog needing to quench his thirst and relieve his dry mouth.

Attention-seeking puppies and young dogs quickly learn to whine or bark when separated from an owner by a closed door or when shut outdoors. If an owner rushes to open doors when a dog calls, the puppy soon understands that this behaviour will trigger an owner's reappearance. Once an over-dependent condition develops, repeated vocalization is often the early indication of the onset of separation-related disorder.

Any howling your dog creates in your absence is him calling to you wolf-style. The wolf ancestor in him triggers an innate calling behaviour that has been used by canines for millions of years. Wolves are known to climb to an elevated position on a mountainside and call across the night-time valley. A lone male wolf may do this to call to a mate or challenge other males.

HOW CAN I TELL IF MY DOG IS UNHAPPY AT BEING SEPARATED FROM ME?

It can be extremely useful to video your dog's behaviour, placing a camcorder on a tripod and filming from the time you go through the motions of leaving your dog and home and during the initial period of absence, as we know that this is the critical time. If this is not possible, another successful method is to set up an audio recorder. Initial displays or sounds of anxiousness and vocalization and scratching will be recorded and this information may even indicate the degree of the condition suffered by your dog. Filmed evidence of dogs with separation-related disorder has revealed that they show the same emotional reaction whether they have been left for five minutes or five hours – it is the immediate loss of contact that is the crucial factor. Mondays are often the worst days because dogs have had plenty of attention including special walks over the weekend.

SIGNS OF SEPARATION-RELATED DISORDER

There are four distinct behavioural signs of the condition:

• Repeated barking, whining or howling

• Toileting in the home

• Obsessively chewing non-edible items, including vinyl floor coverings, digging or scratching at doors and doorframes and shredding bedding or damaging household items such as furniture

• Stress grooming – repetitive licking or nibbling of the front paws or body

There are several ways of successfully dealing with this condition, including temporarily modifying your relationship with your dog, reducing the cues that lead up to you leaving him alone and making separation less stressful for him. Once he has become more accustomed to being left alone, you can gradually return to a normal relationship.

Dealing with separation-related disorder

HOW TO REDUCE SEPARATION CUES

Your routine patterns of behaviour announce in various ways to your dog that you are leaving him to go to work, shopping or out for the evening, so you need to spend time considering all these tell-tale actions and take steps to avoid them. In the first few weeks you may not see the benefit of these changes, but eventually they will become key to rehabilitation.

• Avoid using repeated word instructions, such as 'See you later', 'Be a good boy' or 'I won't be long'. Avoid all spoken words and leave as discreetly as possible.

• Have clothes, hats, coats, keys and shoes all ready in advance. Conceal yourself in another room when changing. From time to time, put a coat on, handle your keys and remain in the home.

• Don't offer chews, treats or 'interactive toys' the moment you are about to leave (see below).

• Avoid routinely switching the television or radio on or off at bedtime and prior to leaving home. Change your daily listening times when possible.

• Mask or avoid the sound of your home alarm, starting of the car engine, setting answer machines or opening and closing garage doors.

COMFORT MEASURES

Background voices help to reduce hyper-alertness in nervous dogs. Leave a television or radio talk programme playing in the background before, during and after you leave and return home so that the on/off trigger cannot be linked to absence.

Make a toy, chew or a raw, uncooked bone available 30 minutes before you leave, to be discovered after you have left home, to help reduce any potential boredom. Also, when a dog licks a chew or bone, he is calmed by the repetitive action. If he is not indoor kennelled or crated, try giving him an interactive self-rewarding toy such as a foraging ball. These should always be removed a short period after your return in order to maintain their novelty value. Use them at times when you are at home to prevent them being linked to your absence.

SETTING UP A 'DEN'

You will need an indoor crate or bag-style canvas unit tall enough for your dog to stand up in, but not too large to allow exercise or hyperactivity, and a

cover, either purpose-made or a heavy linen cloth. Place the dog's bedding inside, including an item of your clothing that will carry your scent as a comfort blanket, and leave the crate door open. Here your dog can then curl up, relax and rest. Visual stimuli are reduced to a minimum and there can be no guarding, leaping up or barking at passers-by.

INTRODUCING AND
USING THE 'DEN'
Introduce your dog to the den with the minimum of fuss. Ideally, leave the dog in the room where you have placed the unit or step away and allow exploration. If your dog initially ignores the crate, secretly place an enticing bone or new toy inside and then give your dog time and privacy to investigate. The best time of day to experiment with the crate is night-time,

when the dog would naturally be relaxing and usually ready to rest. Allow at least a week or more of introduction time, giving your dog plenty of time to explore and settle in the den. The more relaxed and confident your dog is when entering and leaving the folding crate, the better. Overnight use is vital for long-term success. Only close the crate door when you are confident that your dog is calm within its boundaries.

The den should *never* be used for punishment or visits to the veterinary surgery (certainly not in the early days), to avoid any potential negative association. It should be used as a familiar refuge if you move house, travel in a vehicle or stay in a caravan or boat on holiday, or when taking your dog to other homes or premises. Don't feed your dog his normal daily feed in the den.

Above: *A chew helps to calm a dog. Hide one for your dog to discover after you have left the house and it will soothe his nerves.*

Destructive behaviours

When a dog left alone in the home for a short period scratches, chews or digs, it indicates that he feels somehow trapped, and when you return home to see a floor covered in shredded papers, it may look like wanton vandalism, but it is your dog's way of dealing with the stress of separation.

Stress-related scratching

A dog that is suffering from separation-related disorder will not want to be left behind no matter how brief the time his owner is away from him and the home (see pages 118–119). Once his owner has left, the dog begins to scratch the door that he knows his owner has just gone through, forgetting to take him along. Normally, when an owner sees or hears their dog scratching the door, they open it. Knowing that scratching the door has worked before, the dog believes it will work again. But the door remains shut, so the dog scratches more frantically until his behaviour changes from panic to manic. His scratching then becomes a 'stereotypical' behaviour – a stereotyped, repetitive and non-functional movement (see pages 148–149). Consequently, the dog begins to receive a reward in the form of hormones such as dopamine and serotonin and this temporarily comforts him. But when the hormonal fix recedes, he starts the process all over again.

Destructive chewing

When dogs have finished attacking the door barrier, many appear to accept that there is no way out. Those that are over-dependent on their owners if given the run of the home will begin to search all the rooms where the doors have been left open. Some will seek out items of clothing or footwear, as though they need the access to their owner's scent. When located, these items may be taken to the dog basket to be possessed or he may begin chewing. Just as with repeated door scratching, the dog gains a hormonal reward as the chewing becomes the single focus of his attention. Gentle licking and chewing can develop into manic behaviour, and owners may return home alarmed to find that a best pair of shoes have been shredded.

Others may target furniture, and owners have reported whole sofas that have been ripped to shreds or beds and bedding virtually destroyed, such is the power of manic, hormone-rewarded behaviour. Such dogs when left outside begin digging as a displaced behaviour. Dogs have been known to swallow plastic, wood, socks, underwear and even mobile phones, and the subsequent intrusive surgery only adds to the stress factor that is driving the dog to perform this action.

Early chewing

It is, however, perfectly normal for a dog under six months of age to chew. As his early pin-sharp teeth develop, so too does his urge to chew. If having been provided with items to chew, such as hide chews or toys or hard nylon toys, he targets inappropriate household items, for example, furniture and shoes, action is needed in the form of training discs to signal non-reward (see page 75). When he then chews on an appropriate item, reward him with fuss and attention. If he continues to chew beyond the early teething stages, this may indicate that stress-related, obsessive behaviour is developing (see pages 148–149).

Above left: *Home-alone dogs may seek out owner-scented items during separation and footwear is a popular target.*

Right: *Any destructive behaviour displayed by dogs when separated from family members is not vandalism, but a stress-related condition.*

SHOULD I PUNISH MY DOG OR DO I NEED TO SHOW HIM MORE LOVE?

Punishment only creates more fear of separation and additional stress, while more cuddles and strokes only serve to reinforce his attachment to you. In this situation, kindly owners recognize that the behaviour is not the dog's fault and seek help. Others, perhaps at the end of their own acceptable levels of stress, wonder if re-homing to someone who can be at home with the dog all day would be the best option. Some dogs are re-homed repeatedly, but with the guidance of a qualified animal behaviourist, this condition is treatable.

Inappropriate toileting

Any inappropriate toileting occurring in the home when a dog is left alone is rarely about physical need but an instinctive urge to mark his territory during a period of stress prompted by owner separation. A dog performing this behaviour receives 'chemical relief' in his brain.

How and why it occurs

Inappropriate toileting is not to be confused with difficulties in house-training puppies, sometimes caused by early removal from the mother. Research involving dogs suffering from separation-related disorder (see pages 118–119) has revealed that many dogs urinate or defecate the moment after their departing owners shut the front door. Filmed evidence has shown that this behaviour is common among dogs with the condition and the human parallel is probably bed wetting in children. This situation is seen as a subconscious act and is often an emotional response to the problems they are facing in their lives. A dog will feel temporarily satisfied when his inner territory, which is represented by the home, includes his scent. This is because both urine and faeces are instinctively used as marking scent (see page 84).

Possible causes

Over-dependency combined with territorial insecurity can trigger a dog to seek relief in urinating and defecating indoors. It is very rarely a need to go to the toilet, and it isn't 'dirty behaviour' as we may think of it in human terms. A dog experiencing stress, especially one that has made a strong attachment to his owner, receives a 'chemical relief' in his brain every time he marks and can become addicted to this feeling.

The more attention given to a dog with the condition, the more his distress will increase when his owner is absent. A dog can be unsettled through being given too much petting and close physical contact by a doting owner. Dogs naturally attempt to 'over-mark' each other (see pages 80 and 84) and this can promote a cycle of marking when there is more than one dog in the home. Exposure to any human family anxiety or stress can also trigger inappropriate toileting behaviour.

Owner-attachment issues and elements of territorial insecurity (often seen in rescued or adopted dogs) can trigger a dog to seek some aspect of relief from stress by urinating or defecating in the 'inner-territory' or the home. The use of the den-effect in a time-out zone whilst an owner is at home, can help a dog become used to separation periods. In the meantime it is advisable to restrict or reduce the opportunities that he has to urinate or defecate during owner-absence (either overnight or during the periods he is home-alone) if a speedy solution is to be achieved. This is because, each time a dog marks indoors – especially during owner separation – the action promotes or reinforces the behaviour and any potential 'addiction' to marking is satisfied. Great care must be taken by owners if a separation-related toilet issue is not to be reinforced. It is important that punishment is avoided at all costs and that any mess cleaning should not be undertaken in view of the dog.

Above: Puppies will naturally have the odd accident but regular toilet problems during owner separation are usually a sign of canine insecurity.

Right: If a dog that has toilet issues during owner-separation periods urinates or defecates in an appropriate place this should be rewarded by praise, food treats or clicker sessions.

HOW SHOULD I DEAL WITH MY DOG WHEN I RETURN HOME TO FIND HE HAS MADE A MESS?

It is important to deal with this behaviour very carefully, otherwise the stress experienced by your dog will increase.

Initially, restrict the areas where marking can occur by keeping a dog to one room and place obstructions such as large cardboard boxes in the way of favoured corners. Clean any soiled area thoroughly with a biological spray cleaner, rather than strong disinfectant, to mask his scent and reduce the dog's desire to over-mark the original soiling place. Never clean up any urine or faeces in view of your dog. It is also vital not to shout at or scold your dog for soiling in the home, as he cannot properly associate your reaction with the past event and it will only increase his distress.

Choose a convenient area in the garden to encourage your dog to urinate or defecate. For the first few weeks of this therapy, do not over-clean the area and encourage your dog to visit and use it after a walk (by using a clicker – see page 74), in the morning or just before bedtime at night. Reward your dog for any use or exploration of this area with a 'click and treat', special food treat or a pat and verbal praise.

Transfer any faeces or urine-soiled paper (use kitchen paper to mop up some urine) from the home to the chosen toileting area, as your dog will 'associate' with the freshest scents.

Noise sensitivity

It is well known that dogs have sensitive hearing and that they can detect a range of higher-pitched sounds than we can. If they have developed a hyper-alert state or problems with over-attachment to their owner, dogs can panic at noises so insignificant that we would not feel the slightest need to investigate.

How and why it occurs

Noise sensitivity in dogs can be a part of feeling insecure and lacking in confidence in dealing with ordinary events in daily life, and a wide range of distinctive sounds can become extremely threatening to a nervous dog. It is often first-time experiences of violent sounds, such as loud fireworks, cars backfiring or industrial noise, that have a significant, long-lasting effect on some dogs. Harmless domestic noises. ranging from the window cleaner putting his ladders against the outside wall to the pinging of a microwave oven can also be linked to fear in some dogs' minds.

Once a negative association with a particular sound has been formed – and this need only be once – it can prove extremely difficult to change that connection in a dog's mind.

Above: Terriers can be sensitive to unusual sounds and often take a higher position in the home to guard and target-bark at any sounds or movement outside.

Right: Noise sensitivity in dogs can trigger the fight or flight responses, when crouching down low or crawling behaviour may be witnessed.

Above: Dogs' senses are heightened in the open and once a negative association has been made to certain noises on a walk it can be difficult to treat a panic response.

This is especially true when the negative association has occurred during a walk or when the dog is alone at home when his awareness is heightened. Sound association can work in the opposite way with non-nervous dogs, as when gundogs become desensitized to loud shotgun bangs in hunting game through positively linking the noise to working or training.

Panic responses

On hearing the offending noise, a panic or 'fight and flight response' (see pages 24–25) can be triggered in the dog. This can range from crouching down low, crawling, running away or hiding under beds and other furniture. If the feared sound, such as thunder is heard outdoors, a dog may even refuse to go on a walk.

QUESTIONS AND ANSWERS: SCARY SOUNDS

Should I stroke my dog when he is frightened of a particular noise until he has calmed down?
Noise sensitivity in dogs cannot be overcome by petting and stroking or by offering concerned attention. In fact, this human caring response will often make matters worse by reinforcing or supporting the dog's distress. The owner's kind, reactive behaviour may even suggest to a dog that they are also disturbed and made anxious by the same sound.

How should I help my dog when he is frightened of noises?
It can help to expose your dog to continual sounds in the home and wherever you are staying. If possible, have a talk radio programme playing fairly loudly in the background or gradually raise the volume to mask other noises. It can also help to make durable chews and uncooked bones or foraging/treat ball toys available to distract and help reduce potential hyper-alertness. Try playing short retrieval games that are food-rewarded. It is also important to offer him a 'den' (see pages 120–121), to which he can retreat when he hears a frightening sound. Initially, the bolthole can be a temporary unit such as a large cardboard box.

Should I play recordings of 'scary sounds' at low levels to get my dog used to these noises?
Methods used in the treatment of human phobias, such as continually exposing the phobia sufferer to the focus of their fear, known as 'flooding', have not achieved success when used on dogs. Research has shown that the more a nervous dog is exposed to the cause of his fear, the more likely it is that a 'flight' reaction, i.e., a search for a bolthole, will be triggered. Seeking out or creating a place of refuge or burrow is instinctive canine behaviour (see pages 38–39).

An overly strong attachment to an owner (see pages 114–115) and underlying hyper-alertness (see pages 116–117) are often the reasons why ordinary household noises make a dog fearful. Once the strategies for reducing a dog's alert levels have been in place for some months (see above), it is then a good idea to play retrieval games as a form of distraction, using the clicker to signal reward (see page 74), while low-level recordings of the feared sounds are played in the background.

Flashpoint aggression

Dogs can suddenly turn from being a companion to a threat. Analysing why an aggressive action has occurred in the home and knowing how best to deal with this often unexpected behaviour is the key to understanding a confused dog.

When it occurs

Flashpoint aggression or challenges occur when a dog is triggered to use antisocial behaviour to gain access to an owner, food or toys. Attacks can happen when it is least expected, such as when dogs take up a higher position on stairs or on furniture to show dominance. When there is more than one dog in the home, some acts of aggression often happen around thresholds, in confined spaces or at gateways, or when dogs are getting in and out of vehicles.

Why it happens

It can be hard to come to terms with the fact that a companion dog has just growled or snapped at a family member or stranger. When challenging dogs growl possessively over a toy, it can be difficult to separate what is innocently playful from unacceptable behaviour. A play growl should be higher in tone than a real growl. However, a dog growling over his food bowl is not to be accepted lightly. In some dogs, issues over food have roots in the litter stage and it is known that puppies from large litters where there is over-competition for food have a tendency to become protective or possessive over food as they mature.

Antisocial behaviour is not uncommon in rescue and adopted dogs, and the reasons for the aggression may be related to experiences of abuse or when the dog has been a stray and has had to go without food for periods. When dogs are both nervous and excited the outcome is often aggression. The calmer a dog is the more likely that aggression can be countered or controlled before the behaviour rapidly turns from growling to biting.

WHAT SHOULD I DO WHEN MY DOG GROWLS OR IS SHOWING AGGRESSION?

This can happen when you are removing a food dish, when the dog sees another dog, over instructions such as 'Come down off the furniture', recall, giving up a toy or item or when you wish to remove him from or to another room.

It is important that you don't confront him directly by making eye contact or lowering yourself to his head or height, or talking to or shouting at him. When you are ready, stand in another place (room or garden area) and call him. Click and treat him for coming to you and as he responds to your 'Sit' instruction (see page 74). This strategy will switch his mode of behaviour from challenging to obedience.

If he stalls and you need to prompt him to respond to your instruction, use a pre-associated reward whistle (see page 75). Always reward him, either with a food treat, stroke, verbal praise or toy, and signal with the clicker when he has been obedient and as he responds to your instructions.

If he is growling in a challenging way, first signal clearly with training discs (see page 75) and say in clear, low-pitched voice 'No'. Once he responds positively, sound the reward whistle and use the clicker to congratulate him for sitting, that is, behaving passively.

Dealing with the behaviour

If you discover your dog lying on the sofa, which he is not allowed to do, and you then instruct him to come down but he growls in response rather than obeying you, he is challenging your leadership from an elevated position. The common response would be to take hold of the dog's collar and drag him down to show him 'who's boss', but this reaction allows any confrontation to take place on a lower level. This physical level can be to the dog's advantage, as his limited mental capabilities mean he could never truly compete with an owner on a psychological level. It is always better to say 'No' in a stern voice (or signal non-reward through the use of training discs, see page 75) and then call your dog into another room.

Some flashpoint acts of aggression in dogs will occur so quickly that it is difficult to be prepared in advance. However, you can be forewarned of an episode by staying on the lookout for any early signs of hyperactivity, challenging behaviour, excessive barking, growling or refusal to obey an instruction.

Far left: Always avoid eye contact with a dog when he is being aggressive as confrontation can aggravate him.

Below: The growl, with teeth bared, is part of dog language that would warn off would-be competitors in nature.

Above: *Dogs can be stimulated by interesting scents in their own or other animals' faeces.*

Far right: *A reward whistle can be used to interrupt or distract your dog after he has defecated, followed by a 'click and treat'.*

Faeces eating

Dogs act in ways that can make us laugh and smile or turn away and grimace. When it comes to your dog taking pleasure in recycling his own waste, it is probably time to call in the dog doctor.

Why it occurs

Faeces eating or coprophagia in dogs is the instinctive recycling of partially digested food. It is a behaviour that occurs naturally in the mother, when she cleans up the waste of her puppies in the early stages. In the wild, in times of food shortage, faecal pellets offer a source of undigested bone or skin to younger members of the pack, which may constitute a life-saving meal.

In our pet dogs, this behaviour can be learned from the mother or from other older dogs. It also occurs among puppies that have been raised in an impoverished environment. Another trigger can be the availability of the faeces of other dogs, cats, horses and smaller pets during the litter and post-litter stage up to adulthood. It can also be linked to illness or boredom, or dissatisfaction with an existing diet, as well as to situations where a dog has made a powerful attachment to an owner and is then distressed enough by their absence to toilet in the home (see pages 124–125).

Some professionals advise a change in diet to include food that is high in fibre and protein and low in carbohydrates. However, if a dog is currently enjoying a balanced and varied diet, then nutritional issues are unlikely to be the true cause of the problem.

Owner responses

Faeces eating is probably high on any owner's list of unacceptable behaviour in their dog. Some show a lack of understanding to the point of extremeness, such as resorting to euthanasia, as veterinary records testify, and the severity of this reaction may be provoked by the thought that, having eaten faeces, a dog may well lick a person's face. Owners can unwittingly become part of the problem, as in response to their dramatic disapproval, dogs quickly learn to be more discreet when performing the act, and owner intervention can even cause them to speed up in their move from defecating to eating, since, in the dog's perception, the owner is competing for the same faeces.

Countering coprophagia requires a great deal of patience and understanding. If it is dealt with correctly, this unsettling behaviour can be changed and a healthy interactive situation between owner and dog re-established.

HOW DO I STOP MY DOG BEHAVING IN THIS WAY?

There are several aversion methods that you can employ when your dog turns to inspect his own faeces, to give the action a negative association, some more humane than others. Perhaps the best option is to invest in a remote-controlled scent collar (see page 74). Your dog will quickly associate the overwhelming scent with his behaviour and consequently will reduce or often cease coprophagy altogether.

If you spot the behaviour about to happen after your dog has defecated, sound training discs (see page 75) or, in acute cases, set off the remote-controlled scent collar. After the behaviour has been interrupted, call your dog to you or use a reward whistle and then 'click and treat' for his good response (see page 74).

If you are there when defecation has already occurred in your home or garden, remove the dog out of sight while the faeces are cleaned away. Use a biological spray cleaner rather than a strong disinfectant to mask the scent and

reduce his desire to soil again in the same place. If on a walk, use a favourite squeaky toy or toy on a rope to re-direct the dog's attention while you collect the waste. Try not to make the event exciting or dramatic by making a fuss or becoming angry.

It is important to be patient with your dog. Castigating him for lapses will only increase his distress and may even promote a false sense of competition in your dog (see above).

If the faeces eating is occurring in your absence, you may need to use an indoor crate or canvas-style unit (see page 121) in conjunction with professional behavioural advice.

Hiding away

Dogs naturally belong in groups and, just like most humans, they need to be a part of a family or social pack. When a dog withdraws from family life, it is an indication that he is uncomfortable in his world and cannot cope with day-to-day events. The causes of this behaviour are varied.

How it happens

There are dogs that display nervousness from the moment they become part of a family. This generally nervous behaviour, which can at first be viewed as shyness, then develops into cowering under tables or chairs when visitors arrive or flinching when a person moves a limb unexpectedly. Some dogs even urinate in an act of submission when faced with people, while others crawl on all fours as though they expect to be punished without any reason.

Why it occurs

If an otherwise healthy puppy behaves in this way, it indicates a general lack of sociability that has been caused by something untoward occurring at the litter stage. Perhaps the mother herself was insecure or her puppies were taken from her too early. Sometimes it can be the result of the puppy being initially raised in an unsuitable environment, such as pet shops, puppy farms and large commercial outlets, but it can also be seen in farm-raised dogs that have only known a working relationship in a farming context and are therefore far better suited to that environment than living in a home.

When dogs retreat from their owners and everyday family interaction and hide away from everything other than the bare necessities, it is a sure sign that their confidence in the social structure in which they are living has somehow been lost. The recommended course of action is to consult a veterinary surgeon and then be referred to an animal behaviourist for treatment.

Above: Nervous dogs will seek out confined spaces, such as behind an armchair or the sofa, as a safe retreat.

Right: An unhappy dog needs to be gently encouraged to participate in family life with rewarded interaction.

WILL PETTING MY DOG MAKE HIM FEEL ANY BETTER?

When a dog begins to withdraw from being with his family, it means that he isn't enjoying life. Dogs don't stroke each other, so this caring action from an owner rarely helps to bring a hiding companion back into the fold.

Dogs that are hiding away need a suitable bolthole within which they can feel safe. The setting up of a 'den' in the home is the best way to replicate a natural retreat (see page 120). In the 'den', the dog can feel protected from potential threats, whether they are real or imagined.

It is also a good idea to observe on what occasions your dog is even remotely enjoying himself and build on this positive aspect by introducing specially rewarded interaction. If he only appears to be happy when out on walks, try introducing several shorter, 15-minute walks instead of taking him on one long walk. You can then encourage him to play short retrieval games on the walks, offering him enticing food rewards for performing well, which can be linked to the sound of a clicker (see page 74).

If your dog is particularly treat orientated, you could also turn his daily meals into foraging games where he has to search for food partially hidden in the home or garden (see page 89). Once a dog can be seen enjoying some form of canine hedonism, you can then concentrate on preventing any withdrawn behaviour by focusing on these pleasure-inducing activities.

Over- or under-feeding

Dogs can occasionally develop eating disorders, just like owners. If they become fussy eaters or lose interest in food and there are no physical reasons for the behaviour, it could point to a psychological cause. Dogs can also just as easily become overweight if they are offered all the food they can eat or an unhealthy diet.

Fussy feeders

Dogs can quickly learn that they might be offered alternatives if they ignore what is still in the dish and this can lead to fussy eating. Staring pleadingly at you is sometimes enough to get you to open another can or packet. Dogs that are fed tasty human titbits or share in our fast food laced with taste enhancers often become bored with their own specially formulated food. In some ways, it can be like offering a child the choice of a chocolate bar or broccoli; most would not choose the healthier option, and dogs are no different. Prepared dog foods contain the correct balance of ingredients, and it is unhealthy to offer an adult dog excessive amounts of protein (meat, cheese or chicken) or unsuitable foods.

Losing weight

Dogs that have lost the desire to eat heartily have either developed a negative association with food or are suffering from a lack of appetite linked to a psychological disorder, which produces the same effect as anorexia in humans. Making feeding time more interesting can increase a dog's appetite and food-foraging games (see page 89) can help in this respect where a dog would have to search out the latest dish of meat and biscuits. Working dogs will usually have had to 'round up sheep', retrieved the game bird or guarded the perimeter fences before being fed. Your dog can be encouraged to 'work' before obtaining food through firstly being tasked or through agility and foraging games.

Dogs that are offered human foods containing salts and sugars to improve the flavour can lose their taste for formulated dog foods. If they are then walked over long distances, this can lead to dramatic weight loss. Until a dog has regained some weight, the length of his walks should be reduced. All dogs, but especially those with acute weight loss, should be fed after a walk to enable them to rest and properly digest their food.

Above: Obesity in dogs can lead to major organ failure and associated health issues. An overweight dog should be put on a closely controlled diet.

Left: A dog that walks away from his food may be showing a preference for human foods, which could lead to fussiness and even canine anorexia.

Hungry dogs

In nature, a hungry dog cannot know when or where his next meal is coming from, and so when food is plentiful, he usually eats as much as he can. In a similar way, domesticated dogs with a healthy appetite can eat voraciously. However, an increased appetite can trigger the need to eat excessively until obesity begins to affect a dog's health.

If all a 'greedy dog' has to do to eat is visit a food bowl, especially one permanently filled with dried food, he will increase in weight. It is best to offer fixed amounts of food at one or two designated mealtimes rather than allow a dog to eat his whole ration in a single session.

Excessive weight gain can go unnoticed, especially when the increase occurs gradually over many months. Obese dogs need not only to eat less but to be carefully exercised and their weight regularly monitored at a veterinary clinic until the appropriate body mass for their breed and sex has been achieved. Older dogs that enjoy shorter walks can be introduced to a reduced protein food to encourage a healthy weight balance.

Below: *Take a dog for a walk to work off his surplus energy before offering him his daily food.*

QUESTIONS AND ANSWERS: FEEDING ISSUES

What should I do if my overweight dog is over-feeding?
First, establish the correct daily amounts of food to suit the age and breed of your dog with your veterinary clinic. Divide this amount into three feeds. Try to make your dog work for his feeds. Only offer food after a walk, however brief. Show your dog the dish of food and, leaving him inside at the back door, go outside and hide the dish. Open the door and instruct your dog to search for his food.

My dog is not interested in food. How do I encourage him to eat?
Make sure that the food you are buying is appealing and appropriate for your breed of dog. Always offer food after exercise. Reduce feeding treats and any human titbits. Spice up his normal daily diet by adding small amounts of warm, blanched, fatty minced meat (about tennis-ball size for medium to large breeds and half that for small breeds).

Try to make feeding an exciting event. Move the position of the dish on a daily basis (if the weather is good, offer it outdoors) and use a clicker or reward whistle (see pages 74–75) to announce the serving of food.

Above: It is essential that a dog being exercised off-lead in public places is instantly controllable to avoid safety issues with strangers and other dogs.

Protective aggression

Your dog normally views off-lead encounters with people and other dogs on walks with a simple interest. In a dominant or nervous dog, this can translate into an overwhelming need to investigate and circle anything that, at least from his perspective, represents a potential threat to you and to him.

How and why it occurs

When out on walks with your dog, in his view you are hunting and foraging together. The walk can be an exciting affair when off-lead in a rural setting where something new can be just around the next corner, or a less-interesting session on the lead along urban streets. If a carefree, relaxed stroll is your idea of a walk, your dog will usually follow and treat each person or dog encountered in a sociable way without any fear. But in situations where the owner is apprehensive – either about his own dog's behaviour when meeting other dogs or strangers or about their behaviour towards him and his dog – a need to be protected can be projected on to the dog. This transfers the power of protection and control to the dog, which can prompt him into behaving in an antisocial way.

This behaviour is commonly seen in breeds that have a strong guarding or herding instinct, such as the Bull Mastiff, Dobermann Pinscher, German and Belgian Shepherd Dogs, Rottweiler and Border Collie. Originally line bred for their protective or controlling abilities, these breeds can quickly pick up on the apprehensiveness of an owner, most likely through a combination of human body and scent language. The dog then has to make a decision either to protect or ignore the potential threat.

HOW CAN I STOP MY DOG FROM RUNNING OFF AND CHECKING OUT OTHER DOGS OR STRANGERS ON WALKS?

Always carry an object that can be used as a point of focus for your dog, such as a favourite toy from home. Use it first around the home or garden and sound a reward whistle to announce a game (see page 75). Offer a special food treat each time he retrieves the item. At the end of the session (no more than a few minutes), remove the item and keep it only for walks.

Ask a friend to play the role of stranger (with and without a dog of their own) 'armed' with training discs (see page 75). When your dog runs to the role player, they should sound the discs, while at the same time you sound the reward whistle.

If your dog continues to display hyperactivity or aggression, introduce a remote-controlled scent collar as an aversion device (see page 74) and ask your veterinary surgeon for a referral to a registered animal behaviourist.

Off-lead events

All dogs put in a situation where they can detect the apprehensiveness of their owner on a walk will naturally show a willingness to protect the pack leader and thus keep the social bond intact. Some dogs with a positive personality, particularly those that have had the benefit of basic training, will wait and see if their owner displays any challenging behaviour, and if not, the walk can continue without incident. If an owner becomes animated for any reason, then the dog's desire to protect can escalate. In this instance, an off-lead dog may run ahead in order to circle and growl at the approaching target until he is recalled by the owner. If response to recall is poor (see pages 102–103), some dogs will circle nearer until they can judge the potential reaction of the person or dog. Some breeds will even nip or bite.

On the lead scenario

Dogs in a similar situation that are restrained on a lead will rear up on to their hind legs and may even lunge forwards. A lungeing dog can quickly be brought to heel with a padded head-control collar, such as the Dogmatic, the benefits of which, as opposed to a body harness, are universally acknowledged by animal behaviourists. It operates on the same basis as a halter for a horse: if the dog pulls, the head collar effectively turns his head to one side and therefore he cannot move ahead.

If your dog's lungeing behaviour while out on walks is out of control it is also possible to introduce and use corrective methods, such as a compressed air canister (to counter the behaviour) and clicker (to reward or reinforce a more acceptable response). Ask a friend to use the hand-held spray before the dog jumps and be ready to reward a positive change in behaviour.

Below: It is antisocial to allow a dog to lunge or jump up at strangers when in public places. Intensive scenario-training can address this behaviour.

Above: Head collars have proved to be very successful in helping to control a nervous or pulling dog.

Far right: Establishing walk scenarios where your dog encounters other dogs can be useful and will help in retraining.

Stranger and dog aggression

A dog that displays uncontrollable aggression, whether it is dominant, fear-based or protective, towards strangers or other dogs is a serious liability for any owner. Frequently, owners of such dogs simply adapt their walking habits accordingly. This strategy is purely avoidance and won't help to change the antisocial behaviour.

How and why it happens

Contented, secure dogs with a laid-back personality that have never had the experience of being attacked by another dog or been chased off or abused by a stranger, will always view potential encounters in a positive way (see pages 96–97 and 100–101). If, on the other hand, a dog has been attacked by another dog, his defences will be naturally raised and he may develop a 'get in first' strategy. With hackles raised and body line rigid, this dog will often challenge or attack other dogs without any other warning.

Nervous and aggressive dogs on walks could be described as 'loaded guns' because they are in a heightened state of arousal or readiness. This increased alertness ensures that even more adrenaline, needed for the 'fight or flight response' (see pages 24–25), temporarily floods into the dog's brain.

Research reveals that a dog's decision to chase off or attack another dog or stranger may be linked to the breed, sex, colour and size of the latter. A stranger may appear threatening if he is wearing a dark coat or a hat, or if he is walking with a stick. Dogs form instant associations because, in nature, they have to remember which is the deadly snake or poisonous prey. Next time it may kill, so a 'second chance' or experience is very important to dogs.

Changing a dog's aggressive behaviour on walks

Ask a friend of neighbour who owns a non-aggressive dog to help you with a retraining programme. Using a calm dog and owner in a controlled scenario will show your dog that not all dogs or people are threatening. Choose an unknown territory that is neutral ground for both dogs. The more factors in the scenario that you can control when encountering other dogs

A CONTROLLED WALK

Walks offer an ideal opportunity for developing a controlled bond between you and your dog.

1 First, give your dog a short controlled walk away from the neutral place you have chosen for the encounter. If he is nervous when you are near to roads, people or other dogs, instruct your dog to sit and 'click and reward' with a pat, food treat and/or verbal praise (see page 74).

2 Encourage him to sit several times and reward obedience with reassurance and a click, sometimes followed by a food treat.

3 When the other dog has first come into sight, slacken your hold on the lead and remain relaxed. Any apprehension you feel is directly transmitted to your dog through the lead and by hormonal signals. With your dog clearly under your control (sitting), offer a further reward (several clicks and treats or a toy) as the other dog is walked towards your dog (side on) and past him about 10 m (11 yd) away. Keep your dog in a sideways-on position to the other dog. This will prevent him from appearing dominant to the other dog and should not provoke the other dog to be aggressive. Repeatedly sound

the clicker, without a food treat, with a one-minute pause between each click, to give your dog a continuing reward for his appropriate behaviour and to distract him. You may need to use a special toy to capture his attention or a reward whistle or ball linked to special food treats to maintain his interest and exercise control. Praise all appropriate behaviour. Ignore any excitement, as your attention can inadvertently reinforce and reward your dog's unwanted behaviour.

4 Move the dogs in adjoining circles where they are closely exposed to each other, and 'click and treat' all good behaviour. Gradually decrease the distance between the dogs if they are showing positive behaviour.

5 Try to end the session on a positive note, before your dog has displayed any excitability or aggression. Praise and 'click and treat' him freely for good behaviour.

Repeat the sessions as frequently as possible, gradually reducing the distance between the dogs until they can pass within 1 m/yd of each other without showing aggression. Training discs should be used to signal to your dog that he must stop any inappropriate behaviour (see page 75).

or strangers, the better the chance you have of changing your dog's usual response.

It is important to start the session in a calm manner. Have all the items and clothing you need ready in advance to reduce any hyperactivity and frustration in the dog that will be increased by delay. If a dog is over-excited before a walk, his adrenaline levels will affect his general behaviour and will also potentially increase the degree of aggressiveness. The dog should initially be on a short, strap-type lead combined with a padded head-control collar (see page 137). If your dog is powerful and has previously displayed extreme aggression towards other dogs, use a muzzle.

Chasing livestock

Dogs can instinctively respond to livestock as a wild predator would towards prey. This behaviour has been selectively bred for in working breeds and can be seen in Border Collies and cross-breeds with a collie influence, German and Belgian Shepherd Dogs and in many terrier breeds.

It occurs in some dogs because they lack the stimulation they would have received in fulfilling their traditional working roles as a gundog, sheep herder, fighter, guard or rodent hunter, for which they were originally bred. Research suggests that the behaviour can also have its origins in a lack of social

Above: When a dog is exposed to livestock it is important to praise and reward him with a pat or a food treat when he behaves well.

interaction or a poor environment during the early development period leading into sexual maturity. Some dogs learn to chase when living or being walked in rural areas where they are constantly exposed to grazing livestock. They may even be aroused enough to display predatory aggression where they attack and bite the animals, with the risk of being destroyed by the farmer. The behaviour can become extremely addictive in that when the dog sees the livestock and starts to chase in aggressive mode, the 'prey' show the 'flight' response, which reinforces his action and makes the 'game' more exciting.

Canine fixation

There are dogs that have learned to bolt when they are off-lead and first encounter livestock in a rural environment. In these situations, the dog can run moorlands or fields for hours as they become aroused and adrenaline fuelled. Many of these dogs finally find themselves exhausted and disorientated. Lost and hungry dogs in these circumstances are either adopted by the finder or handed in to rescue centres.

If a dog is known for being fixated about livestock on rural walks but needs to be fully exercised in an area where herds or flocks are being grazed, it is important that a strong fitting lead is locked firmly into a head-collar and that a lunge line is used. In this situation, the dog can be released to run but can be quickly roped in when necessary. If such a dog is off-lead and he triggers livestock to run away he is bound by his fixation to give chase. Care in these circumstances can save plenty of searching and much sadness if a dog cannot be found.

HOW CAN I DEAL WITH THE PROBLEM OF LIVESTOCK CHASING?

Aversion methods, such as using a remote-controlled scent collar (see page 74), can be used to associate a negative event with the behaviour and to break the conditioned response between first seeing the livestock and chasing them. The same approach will also help if the chasing behaviour has been transferred to other targets, such as vehicles, skateboards, cyclists and motorcycles.

If a dog refuses to respond or obey a recall, you can use a lunge-type rope – a long, soft fabric rope like that used for schooling horses – (use gardening gloves to prevent rope burn) or a strong extending lead in conjunction with a padded head-control collar (see page 137). This will allow your dog to roam, while using a reward whistle to encourage recall (see page 75). The rope or lead gives you the opportunity to reel the dog in if he refuses to come on your instructions. This level of supervision can be reduced after a few months when the dog has clearly learned new routines and has improved recall during walks.

Below: *The natural curiosity between animals can be encouraged providing there is an absence of hyperactivity or aggression from the dog.*

Health

Warning signs

Whenever a dog's personality alters in a significant way, there is always a cause. Happy, contented dogs don't suddenly take on a *Jekyll and Hyde* split personality. Any sudden change in your dog's behaviour or personality should tell you that something is wrong, but it may not be obvious what stress factors may have caused the change.

What is cause for concern

Knowing what has caused a dog to change from a lively companion to one that skulks in corners or why a pleasant dog has suddenly become aggressive will not treat the problem in itself, but it will help you to understand and begin dealing with the underlying insecurity or influences.

Temporary changes in activity, feeding and sleep patterns should not be a cause for alarm, but if there is a fundamental change in your dog's patterns of behaviour, it may be necessary to check his health. A physical problem may, as a dog ages, become progressively worse, as in the case of the inherited condition hip dysplasia where the ball and socket joints are misaligned. This development would cause gradual mood changes because of aches and pains. A dog that has pulled a leg muscle after a boisterous play session or walk will be subdued, and may limp about and want to rest more. However, the same dog in constant pain from sore limb joints caused by a genetic condition is likely to become generally bad tempered. The earliest signs of a long-term physical disorder may be the odd yelp as the dog jumps down steps or climbs into vehicles. He may even begin to let out a low growl when being stroked.

Managing physical conditions

The difficulty is that a dog can't explain how he feels, but if early signs of health problems or conditions are recognized, a veterinary surgeon can arrange a thorough examination, including taking X-rays or arranging scans. Once a physical problem has been identified, it can be treated or managed accordingly. For example, in the case of hip dysplasia, a programme of pain management can be introduced. The dog's lifestyle can also be modified to help counter such conditions, by giving shorter walks rather than long, strenuous ones, with play sessions that centre around hide-and-seek games and keep physical activity to a minimum. Dogs, just like their owners, need to rest in order to recover from physical injuries or painful conditions.

POSSIBLE INFLUENCES ON BEHAVIOUR

Direct effects on the dog
• Physical problems, such as congenital heart disease, hip and elbow dysplasia, arthritis, epilepsy or acute infections
• Prolonged illness, requiring frequent veterinary visits
• Intrusive surgery, including neutering
• Hormonal, such as when a dog is reaching the age of sexual maturity
• Physical trauma, following a road traffic accident or organ collapse

Family influences
• Changes in family, such as loss of a family member; a new partner moving in/moving in with a new partner
• Change in owner study or work patterns
• Owner illness/hospitalization
• Over-dependency on an owner
• House move
• Introduction of another dog or puppy or other pet
• Owner anxiety, stress and breakdown
• Physical punishment or excessive chastisement

Other influences
• Adoption/rescue
• Abuse by people
• Attack by another dog or other animal
• House fire or break-in
• Fireworks and industrial noises
• Thunder, high winds and heavy rain

PSYCHOLOGICAL–PHYSICAL CROSSOVER SIGNS

As with humans, if dogs are psychologically happy, they are more able to fight off illness, but if they are low in spirit, they are more likely to succumb to infections and viruses. This is because our immune system and theirs are both placed under pressure when mentally stressed. The following are the main physical signs that may arise in such situations:

Signs that may indicate intestinal infections and parvovirus
• Diarrhoea (loose faeces for more than a day) and continual vomiting
• Visible inflammation (redness) or discharge in the eyes or ears
• Discoloured faeces
• Weight loss
• Vomiting (indicates poisoning when accompanied with collapse or twitching)

Signs that may indicate a parasite infection or dermatological allergy
• Excessive scratching
• Baldness

Signs that may indicate eye infections, such as conjunctivitis and glaucoma
• Discharge
• Inflammation and/or swelling
• Blocked tear ducts
• Grey coating and cataracts
• Third eyelid exposed (this is normal in some breeds)
• Redness

Signs that may indicate major organ disease or diabetes
• Excessive drinking of water
• Listlessness
• Loss of appetite
• Weight loss
• Eye discoloration

Signs that may indicate a seizure, heart disease or airway blockage
• Convulsions
• Excessive coughing

Far left: Personality changes in your dog, such as a constant desire to be at your side, can be signs of the onset of a psychological condition.

Below: A veterinary surgeon can usually identify any physical causes for changes in your dog's behaviour.

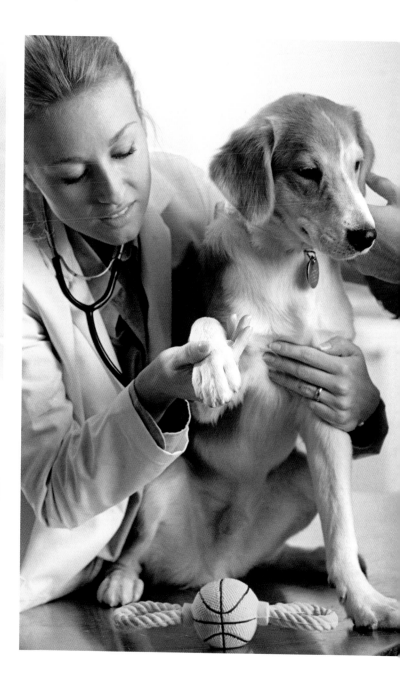

Canine depression and stress

It is not easy to tell whether a dog is suffering from canine depression or stress, because everyone has different expectations in relation to their dogs and the signs are not always obvious, unless they are properly understood. To know if your dog is depressed or stressed, you need to review how he behaves when separation occurs and monitor his reactions to outside influences.

Initial approaches

The causes of canine depression, one of the more unusual health problems in dogs, may not be obvious and there could be many influences. It may be possible for a qualified animal behaviourist to make a preliminary diagnosis and help to identify the triggers. A professional could even offer a behaviour-modification programme to make positive changes. In any case, a referral would normally be made by your veterinary surgeon.

The emotional limp

It is not always the case that a dog with a limp has something wrong with a limb. Research has shown that a dog can learn to use or feign the physical effect of a once-genuine injury to obtain his owner's attention. This 'emotional limp' still needs to be examined in order to ask why it is that the dog needs to use a pretence to obtain attention. A dog that is seeking his owner's attention on a regular basis – beyond the occasional paw or head on your lap – has developed an overly strong attachment to the owner.

Signs of withdrawal

The less obvious sign of the onset of a psychological disorder can be seen when a dog begins to withdraw from normal social family life (see pages 132–133). A dog that takes itself off to hide under beds or furniture when visitors arrive in the home is displaying behaviour that is abnormal in a social animal. Some observers might suggest that this reaction is related to the dog's personality, and dogs can, like humans, be characterized as being introverted or extroverted in temperament. But in any event, dragging an 'introverted dog' back into the living room when visitors arrive will not help to address the problem. A withdrawn dog must be gently coaxed into a more sociable relationship in a positive way through interactive walks and short, well-rewarded play sessions.

Home-alone dogs

Sometimes there is a tell-tale pattern to changes in a dog's behaviour. Dogs that have developed an over-dependency on their owner often react to the sudden post-weekend loss of contact by displaying one or more of a range of problem behaviours – destructiveness, excessive barking and inappropriate toileting – at the beginning of the week (see pages 118–119). Dogs that are experiencing stress often take in lots of water, sometimes following excessive barking, and can be seen drinking far more than is usual.

Not all dogs that are strongly bonded with their owners develop behavioural or psychological problems. They may faithfully follow them from room to room around the home, but they come to learn to accept separation, and simply lie and patiently wait for their owner to return home. It is important to understand that it is only when separation triggers the onset of abnormal behaviours that we need to be concerned.

Stress grooming

An owner would not normally link the action of their dog methodically licking his paw or the inside of his hind legs with stress. This natural behaviour comes from a dog's instinctive desire to keep his coat and skin clean. Also, dogs lick minor scratches clean because of the healing properties in saliva, for the same reason that we would lick a finger cut. But when lick-grooming sessions start to continue beyond a reasonable time period and on a regular, daily basis, this is an indication that the behaviour is developing into obsessive and compulsive disorder (see pages 148–149). The problem may not be apparent if it is a response to an absent owner and so occurs when they are away from home.

Far left: The onset of general apathy or lethargy in young dogs, alongside a withdrawal from social life, is an indication of canine depression.

Below: Watching anxiously as you leave the house, if only for a few moments, indicates a possible fear of separation.

Obsessive and compulsive disorders

Dogs that perform repetitive actions, such as excessive barking, tail chasing or chewing, are suffering from a combination of a neural imbalance in the brain and some degree of canine insecurity.

How and why it occurs

Separation-related disorder is a stress condition and can develop when a dog has formed a powerful attachment to or over-dependency on an owner. There are several triggers including adoption, trauma caused by intrusive surgery, illness or accident, changes in an owner's work patterns, an owner's sudden absence or the loss of a pack member (human or canine), infirmity, nervousness and house moves.

The condition is seen most widely in rescue and re-homed dogs, where, since no one can explain to them why an attachment has been broken, they become afraid of losing another owner. Frequently, most of the problem behaviour occurs in the owner's absence or, in certain cases, when a dog is only visually separated from an owner, such as during night-time sleeping or when shut behind a door. In rare cases, the same behaviour can be shown when family members are in the home, which may, given their presence, disguise the true nature of the problem.

Most owners can easily be forgiven for not recognizing stress in a companion dog for although there are many parallels in human behaviour, many repetitive actions occur when owners are absent. It can be useful to set up a camcorder in a room where a dog remains when family members are not present. Start the camera and leave the room or house for up to 15 minutes. Reviewing the filming can reveal a great deal about how your dog deals with stress.

COMMON REPETITIVE ACTIONS

There are a number of repetitive behaviours that dogs can engage in, including:

• barking
• tail chasing
• reflection chasing
• grooming (licking)
• scratching
• digging
• chewing
• performing circling patterns
• moving from side to side
• air gulping
• chasing any moving target, such as livestock, motorcycles, joggers, etc.

Above left: *Many of the repetitive behaviours that can be seen in dogs, such as scratching, occur as they attempt to deal with the effects of stress.*

Signs of stress and fear

All stereotyped, non-functional, repetitive movements, known as 'stereotypical behaviours', seen in dogs are stress related or fear based, and dogs that display any of the actions in the panel opposite or any other actions repeatedly and excessively have a condition similar to that suffered by humans known as obsessive-compulsive disorder (OCD). Some canine OCD-like behaviours may drive a dog to behave hyperactively towards associated 'cues', for example shadows or reflective lights or sounds such as a doorbell. Obsessive-compulsive behaviour directed towards moving targets or post coming through the letterbox is common among nervous dogs, but there are other dog behaviours that are not always obvious to the observer as obsessive and compulsive.

An association with the 'cue' can then develop in the dog's mind, such as the sound of the doorbell signifying the gaining of attention and excitement in meeting a visitor, or the telephone ring meaning the loss of his owner's attention, which can trigger a wide range of other problem behaviours, from panic, hyperactivity, chasing, target barking and hiding to collapse, destructiveness and even inappropriate toileting.

Left: Dogs that are hyper-alert or nervous can become addicted to barking at visual targets or sounds.

IS THERE ANYWAY TO DEAL WITH CANINE OCD BEHAVIOUR?

Obsessive-compulsive behaviour cannot be overcome by punishing, shouting, excessive petting, stroking or attention. All these responses will often reinforce or support the dog's reactive behaviour. It may even suggest to your dog that you are also disturbed by the object of his attention. It is important to deal with the causes of the behaviour and try to make your dog more secure with you and in his immediate environment, such as by setting up a 'den' (see page 121).

1 When your dog begins any repetitive action, immediately and calmly signal with training discs that have been pre-associated with the removal of a food treat or reward (see page 75). You must try to avoid giving your dog any direct attention such as eye or physical contact or spoken words.

2 If he stops performing the behaviour, immediately sound the clicker that has become associated with a food reward (see page 74), but at this stage don't offer any reinforcing reward (treat, contact or toy). If your dog continues to cease the behaviour, click several times, leaving a one-minute pause between each click.

3 If he resumes displaying the repetitive behaviour, immediately sound the training dics again. Always sound the clicker immediately the problem behaviour ceases, even if it is only momentary. Repeatedly sound the clicker (up to four times, leaving a pause of up to five minutes between each click in the first stages) if he continues to respond and does not resume the problem behaviour.

4 Temporarily prevent him from any excessive guarding and target barking by restricting his access to window views (draw curtains or restrict front-room access), garden gates and doorways until the condition has been successfully treated.

Make sure that you reduce or control any events that may provoke his excitement to any great level because the combined effect of 'reward hormones' and adrenaline that this produces will only increase or reinforce the condition.

Seizure-related behaviour

When a dog is found in a trance-like state, staring ahead as though he has seen a ghost, this rather unusual behaviour is likely to be caused by epilepsy. Some breeds are more prone to suffering from epilepsy than others, and some dogs can fall unconscious following a seizure.

HOW AND WHY IT OCCURS

Epilepsy is usually described as a neurological disorder that can trigger convulsions or seizures. It is known to be linked to a chemical imbalance in the brain and is affected by erratic or unstable neuron or electrical activity.

One of the first indications that a dog is suffering from mild epilepsy is evidence of unusual behaviour. Dogs can be discovered standing unmoving under bushes or furniture looking as though they are in a trance. Dogs have been observed animatedly eating from their food bowl one moment and in the next suddenly standing still as if time itself had come to a stop. In acute cases, dogs will begin breathing heavily and then attempt to seek out a quiet place before collapsing. Usually, after a short period of unconsciousness, the dog will awaken and proceed to drink from a water dish more vigorously than normal.

IN THE BREEDING

There are a number of breeds that are known to be prone to partial or full seizure attacks and these include several of the terrier breeds, especially the less-widely kept ones, such as the English Bull Terrier and the Fox Terrier. However, it is also a condition commonly seen in the different forms of the Belgian Shepherd Dog and, at the other end of the popularity scale, epilepsy is also known to affect breeds such as Poodles, Labradors and Golden Retrievers.

SEIZURES IN DOGS

Although there does appear to be a genetic predisposition for seizures in particular dog breeds it is possible for any dog to develop the imbalance in brain chemistry that can bring on fits. Just as in the human condition, tiredness, stress, hyperactivity and light sensitivity can trigger a fit or seizure.

It is possible to detect early signs of a seizure in a companion dog by noticing any unusual eye-flickering or stumbling. In these circumstances, a dog can be led into a quiet room and put to rest. Dogs can overcome the effects through calmness and rest and often wake up thirsty and ready for action again.

Any dog that is known to be prone to seizure attacks should be played with and exercised carefully with the rule of brief frequent sessions rather than physical or mentally tasking walks or vigorous play.

WHAT TREATMENT CAN I GET FOR MY EPILEPTIC DOG?

Once a vet has diagnosed the condition, it is usually possible to manage it through the use of therapeutic levels of barbiturates (phenobarbitone) given on a daily basis. In the majority of cases, dogs on medication show a reduction in partial seizures and many avoid having a full epileptic fit. Dogs that show signs of 'trancing' (standing still staring into space) or begin staggering prior to a seizure should be given the opportunity to use a 'den' (see page 121) where they can rest until the effects have worn off. It can also be useful to feed the dog on a raised platform because it would appear that the trigger for some mild seizures is when a dog hangs his head down to eat.

If you discover your dog in a trance, sound a reward whistle (see page 75) or squeak a toy to switch his mind set, but then, after offering a food treat, allow the dog a quiet period to rest.

Above: English Bull Terriers are a breed known to be prone to trancing and seizure episodes.

The pregnant bitch

When female hormones are triggered by pregnancy, a range of maternal behaviours may become apparent. If the mating has been accidental, sometimes it is the slightest changes in personality that provide the early signs that a dog is pregnant, and on occasions, confirmation can be made before a veterinary surgeon confirms the condition.

Signs of pregnancy

If your dog has been deliberately mated according to a breeder plan, changes in her personality may be observed before any developing physical signs show the success of the mating session. The first indication that a bitch is pregnant can often be the colloquial observations that she is a bit 'off colour' or 'under the weather'. Owners who are unaware of the condition may notice her being a little more subdued than she would normally be and could link this to the onset of a season.

Depending on the general personality of the dog, a pregnant bitch may become more 'clingy' than normal, especially around female members of the family. This change is linked to a natural cooperation that occurs between females in the feral or wild pack. It is usual for the *alpha* female or lead bitch in the pack to be the only one that breeds and so the other, lower-ranking females support her during pregnancy.

To facilitate this cooperation, intended to ensure that the puppies have the best chance of growing into adults, there is less natural competition between females than male dogs. In nature, many of the status postures seen in male dogs, such as raising hackles and standing rigid and upright to reduce aggression between them, rarely develop in bitches. Perhaps, ironically, this factor is known to create serious inter-bitch aggression in domesticated dogs because insecure pet females don't offer each other these important signals that would help to prevent injury.

Nesting behaviour

The secondary signs that a dog is pregnant can be her sudden interest in seeking out the quietest and warmest corners in the house; she may start to rest more and show a lack of interest in going for walks. Eventually she will begin to display a general restlessness, revealing that something is affecting her. This can include expressing a need to be outdoors, but then wanting to come back indoors immediately, or showing dissatisfaction with any of her regular resting spots and a much-repeated circling before attempting to lie down. Almost

Above: *Pregnant bitches instinctively search out warmth and rest before eventually selecting a nesting place.*

Left: *Although her puppies can be very demanding on a litter-mother in the early stages, she will calmly care for them all.*

all dogs 'circle' before bedding down to rest in an innate behaviour that is thought to be linked to making the ground more comfortable to sleep on and to check it for spiders and snakes.

The next step in her hormonal-driven preparations is when she starts eagerly looking under tables, chairs, beds or even a space between cardboard storage boxes in the utility room. This behaviour is a displacement for seeking out the burrow or den in nature. Professional breeders would usually offer a bitch a nesting box in a quiet room in the home at this stage so that she can become comfortable in what will be the place in which she will give birth to her puppies. Some females reject the birthing place chosen by owners and become even more driven to find a secluded place to make a den of their own choice. Research reveals that this can be under the house if there is a space or beneath outside buildings and sheds. It is not unknown for a stray pregnant dog to be discovered only when her puppies begin to explore outside of the nesting area at about four weeks of age.

Below: Entire bitches can show unusual behavioural patterns in response to hormonal changes during the onset of a season.

PHANTOM PREGNANCY

When a non-pregnant female begins to display den-searching behaviour, it can be a clear sign of what is known as a canine phantom pregnancy. This is where a hormonal imbalance has occurred and a bitch is consequently triggered into a false sense of the early stages of pregnancy. Owners report their dogs scratching furiously at a particular spot on a carpet under tables or beds in an action that suggests they are attempting to dig out a nesting burrow or den. In acute cases where phantom pregnancies are regularly experienced, a vet can prescribe a course of hormonal treatment to help counter the problem.

The ageing dog

The signs of old age in a dog are not very different from those found in humans – grey whiskers and a reduced sparkle in the eyes or the effect of stiff joints. By the time your dog is seven years old, he is already almost 50 years of age in human terms and middle age will be the stepping stone to old age.

Above: An older dog will be very contented to rest by a warm fire in preference to a cold, winter walk.

Right: Dogs that have led active lives go into the twilight of life having enjoyed every social day with their owners.

A time for old age

Scientists now age dogs in human terms by equating their first year to 14 of ours and thereafter seven of ours for every dog year, because most dogs reach sexual maturity within the first year of their lives. This can only be used as a guideline because some large-breed dogs do well to reach the age of ten, whereas many smaller breeds can live until they are 16 or more.

A dog in middle age normally requires less play and fewer walks. The daily walk can be reduced to a gentle stroll to the local shops and back. There will always be an extrovert dog that still wants to jump over walls and fences and race across fields. However, the price to pay for this extended athleticism will potentially be stiff joints, strained muscles and exhaustion.

Tired old bones

The signs of old age in animals are universal. Just like us, the infirm dog may suffer from stiffness and aches and pains. There will be a subtle, general reduction in mobility and vitality. It is at this stage when owners begin to lift their dog in and out of vehicles. Your dog will probably revel in taking long afternoon naps in a sunlit lounge or sleeping by the warm fire on wet and windy evenings. Extended walks may still be enjoyed at the time, but the physical effect will be felt later in old bones and muscles that are more tired and aching than usual.

Where the fur was once strong in colour, greyness may take over and in some long-haired dogs moulting may increase and can even leave bald patches. Some dogs display a marked change in appetite and begin leaving some of their food. Offer less food and ensure that it has lower-protein levels, such as foods specially developed for dogs in old age.

It is not unusual for elderly dogs to develop incontinence and they may even urinate in the home overnight or when left for long periods. In these cases, it is advisable to arrange a urinary check-up with your veterinary clinic. It is important not to punish any dogs for 'accidents', and this is especially true for elderly dogs.

When the end is near

Once your dog has reached about ten years of age, he will be the equivalent of a human octogenarian. He will be slower to react to changes and may be more than content just to allow the world to pass by. Some dogs enjoy their finest hours when they are close to the end. The onset of a terminal decline can be marked by a show of renewed energy and a coat that suggests good health is returning. This could be described as the last throws of life in a hormonal-burst effect that can also sometimes be seen in elderly human patients.

There may come a time when it is obvious that your dog is struggling to fight off the ravages of old age, and your veterinary surgeon can offer professional advice in this situation. You will be greatly attached to your dog and any talk of euthanasia won't come easily to your family. However, it can be a kindness to prevent prolonged suffering. In this instance, it may be wise to talk to a relative who doesn't share your emotional attachment to your canine friend, who may help you over the necessary process. It is always best to fix your mind on a favourite moment or time with your dog than to dwell on the sadness of the end of your relationship. It is right and proper to grieve for your dog, but it is part of gentle healing to remember better times.

BIBLIOGRAPHY

'Population Biology and Ecology of Feral Dogs in Central Italy', Boitani, Francisci, Ciucci and Andreoli, within 'The Domestic Dog: Its Evolution, Behaviour and Interactions with People', edited by James Serpell, Cambridge University Press 1995, reprinted 1997.

'The Effect of Food and Restricted Exercise on Behaviour Problems in Dogs', G. Anderson and S. Mariner, Canine Academy, KwaZulu Natal, South Africa; Zoology Department, University of Durban-Westville, South Africa.

'Genome Sequence, Comparative Analysis and Haplotype Structure of the Domestic Dog', Lindblad-Toh, Wade, Mikkelsen et al, Nature 438, 803–819, December 2005.

ACKNOWLEDGEMENTS

Executive Editor Trevor Davies
Project Editor Charlotte Macey
Executive Art Editor Darren Southern
Designer Geoff Borin
Senior Production Controller Nigel Reed, Carolin Stransky
Picture Research Giulia Hetherington

Author acknowledgements:
I would like to record my appreciation to Trevor Davies for commissioning me to write this special book and for his important editorial guidance in its early stages. My thanks also to Charlotte Macey for keeping me online with a tight publishing schedule and to the design team for putting together a great set of visuals to support my work. Finally, a special thank you to all my referring veterinarians and our clients because it is by treating their wayward dogs that helps in the understanding of not only the companion canine mind but also the specific needs of their devoted owners.

Photographic acknowledgements:
Alamy Aflo Foto Agency 4-5, AM Corporation 49, Arco Images 12, 81, 100, 125 above, 134 above, 137, blickwinkel 85, Bob Jackson 88, Bob Torrez 65, Celia Mannings 70, 71, David Hutt 42, f1 online 122, 129, Heather Watson 107, imagebroker 19, Isobel Flynn 45, Juniors Bildarchiv 60 below, 73 above, 87, 106 below, Khaled Kassem 141, Photo Network 145, Richard Robinson 30, Robert McGouey 64, Ron Hayes 130, Shout 153, Stock Connection Distribution 79, 89, tbkmedia.de 10, 37, 47 above, 69, Wildscape 90; Animal Photograph Sally Anne Thompson 91; Ardea John Daniels 138, 139, 140; Companyofanimals.co.uk 75; Corbis A Inden/zefa 58, Bloomimage 114, Dale C Spartas 67, DLILLC 103, 118 below, Dylan Ellis 47 below, Gabe Palmer/zefa 116, Herbert Spichtinger/zefa 59, Image Source 2, 48, ImageShop 98 below, Jim Craigmyle 60 above, Jose Luis Pelaez Inc 111, Larry Williams 35, LWA-Dann Tardif 40-1, Philip Harvey 16, Renee Lynn 50; FLPA David Hosking 106 above, Angela Hampton 34, 96, David Dalton 135, Foto Natura Stock 152 above, Gerard Lacz 56 above, Jake Eastham 11, Mark Raycroft 13, 14 above, 28 below, Mark Raycroft/Minden Pictures 52, 62, 142-3, 151, Stefanie Krause-Wieczorek 20, 57, 72; Getty Images Altrendo 76-7, altrendo nature 18, BFW/Neovision 92, Blue Line Pictures 144, Cal Crary 108, Christopher Furlong 22, David Sacks 32, Deborah Jaffe 36, Denis Felix 44, Donald Nausbaum 146, Elke Selzle 93, Ghislain & Marie David de Lossy 61, GK Hart/Vikki Hart 134 below, Gone Wild 115, Mark Raycroft 28 above, 29, Martin Rogers 14 below, Martin Ruegner 98 above, Michael Hall 101, Neo Vision 102, 132, Peter Dennen 154, Roderick Chen 78, Safia Fatimi 121, Sharon Montrose 39, Shinya Sasaki/Neovision 83, 147, Sylvain Grandadam 8-9, Terry Husebye 133, Tim Platt 136; istockphoto.com Barry Crossley 125, Hedda Gjerpen 109, Karen Massier 110, Nick Belton 128, Rosemarie Gearhart 149, Tuomas Elenius 118 above; Jetcare.co.uk 74; Jupiterimages Niclas Albinsson 120; Masterfile Alison Barnes Martin 33, 126 above, Burazin 123, Chad Johnston 24, Jerzyworks 68, Mark Tomalty 54-5, Rommel 127, Shannon Mendes 126 below, Steven Puetzer 86; Nature Picture Library Adriano Bacchella 150, Aflo 46, 94-5, Colin Seddon 26, 155, Wegner/ARCO 31, 56 below; NHPA Ernie James 152 below; Octopus Publishing Group 117, 124; Photolibrary.com Andreas Kindler 105, Botanica 43, ImageState 25, Juniors Bildarchiv 21, 66, 73 below, 97, Lori Adamski-Peek 38, Nonstock Inc 15, Ryan McVay 80, Tom Edwards 148; Punchstock 112-3; Robert Crook 131; RSPCA Photolibrary Angela Hampton 104; Science Photo Library Kenneth H Thomas 51; Shutterstock.com Andrzej Mielcarek 84, Devin Koob 7, Joanna Stachowiak 53, Lee O'Dell 23, Patrick McCall 82, Tim Elliott 17.